A Short Book
on the Subject of Speaking

A Short Book

n the Subject of Speaking

JOHN QUICK

Consultant, Senior Professional Staff
Arthur D. Little, Inc.

Illustrated by Donald Doyle

McGRAW-HILL BOOK COMPANY
New York St. Louis San Francisco Auckland Bogotá
Düsseldorf Johannesburg London Madrid
Mexico Montreal New Delhi Panama
Paris São Paulo Singapore
Sydney Tokyo Toronto

Library of Congress Cataloging in Publication Data

Quick, John, date
   A short book on the subject of speaking.

   Edition of 1973 published under title: I hate
to make speeches.
   Includes index.
   1. Public speaking.   I. Title.
PN4121.Q5   1978   808.5'1   77-18140
ISBN 0-07-051050-4

123456789   MUBP   7654321098

Previously published by Grosset & Dunlap under the title
I Hate to Make Speeches. Copyright © 1973 by John Quick.

*The editors for this book were W. Hodson Mogan and Janine Parson,
the designer was Naomi Auerbach, and the production supervisor
was Teresa F. Leaden. It was set in Electra, by Bi-Comp, Incorporated.*

Printed by The Murray Printing Company and bound by The Book Press.

This book is dedicated to my daughter, Margaret.

It is also written in memory of
General George Armstrong Custer (1839–1876).
Let his last engagement serve as a reminder to you.
Learn something about your audience.

Contents

Preface 1

"Use short sentences and be brief."

That was the advice of a speech coach to a recent political candidate. The candidate wanted to run a campaign in which he was forceful, direct, and held people's attention.

It was the greatest advice I'd ever heard.

It is a whole book in just one line.

"Use short sentences and be brief!"

Most speakers won't make the effort to do that. They tend to ramble, and the more they ramble the less interesting and forceful they become.

End of preface.

(P.S. The candidate won.)

Preface 2

I hope I can follow my own advice in writing this deliberately short book on the subject of speaking.

To do so I will condense everything as much as possible and concentrate on readability.

One of the ways to condense ideas is to reduce them to short lists. At the end of this book you will find a series of checklists that summarize the various things you have to worry about when you:

1. Get ready to speak.
2. Speak.
3. Follow up *after* you speak.

(P.S. 2. I encourage you to *use* the checklists, and I would appreciate it if you would physically rip the lists out of the book instead of photocopying them. That way the next reader will have to buy another book, and overall sales will be better. I mention this because I use my mouth not only for speaking but also for eating such things as fried chicken and blueberry pie. Royalties will assure a continuing supply of these consumables.

Thank you for your consideration of this request, destructive though it may seem to you at first.)

Introduction

I will now tell you several things, at least two of which you will remember for a long time, maybe forever:

1. You can get chewing gum out of your hair by rubbing peanut butter on it.

2. The symbol of the Olympic Games, as you know, consists of five interlocking rings. Do you know what they mean? The five rings represent the five continents. The colors have significance, too. They are red, blue, yellow, green, and black—and there isn't a national flag anywhere that doesn't have at least one of these colors in it.

3. People often use the expression "parts per million." Do you have any concept of how much one part per million is? It is 1 inch in 16 miles. It is one minute in two years.

4. You can stop a charging lion by spitting in its mouth.

Now I'll tell you where I got these facts and why I passed them along to you.

It's true. You can stop a charging lion by spitting in its mouth.

1. I was driving along in a car one day listening to the radio when I heard somebody talk about what to do if you ever got chewing gum in your hair. She said that if you rubbed peanut butter on it, the peanut butter would soften the gum. This is because of the oil in peanut butter. You can then remove the peanut butter by shampooing. (And this seems like a much better method than having to cut off a big clump of hair.)

2. The information about the Olympic symbol was mentioned in an impromptu speech I heard recently. Up to that time I didn't know that the number of rings or their color had any particular significance. I immediately thought of the five continents that have athletes living on them, and

tried to think of a flag that didn't have either red, blue, black, yellow, or green in it. I couldn't think of one.

3. Parts per million came up in another impromptu speech. I worked it out with a pencil and paper and, sure enough, it's very close. One inch in sixteen miles. One minute in two years.

4. I'm sorry if the idea of spitting is repellent to some readers, particularly spitting in the mouth of a lion. But I read this information in a book about Africa one time and figured it might be a nice last-ditch thing to know. The lion is said to find the experience very repellent indeed, and it's enough to stop his charge and make him think twice about what he's doing. During that time you might be able to climb a tree or get away. (And even if it proves *not* to be true, I think I would prefer to be remembered by onlookers as follows: "Yes, I was there when John got his head bitten off by the lion. He seemed very brave; just stood his ground and spit in its face.")

Why have I told you these things? Particularly in a book that is supposed to be short.

I'll tell you.

I've been trying to do some of the key things that a talk is supposed to do:

1. Get attention.

2. Use language that you could understand.

3. Concentrate on a limited number of interesting things.

4. Reiterate the key points to help you remember them.

5. And, finally, maybe even commit you to some future course of action (particularly regarding gummy hair or charging lions).

1. First Suggestion: Never Speak to Another Audience

I'm going to lead off with my best piece of advice. Don't get up in front of a group and speak unless (1) you really want to or (2) you absolutely have to.

In every other case, do your damnedest to get out of it. Because chances are that you will fail. There are a lot of reasons for things failing, and we'll talk about them later. In the meantime, however, try to avoid speaking situations.

But suppose, as somebody said to me recently, "You have a chance to be on *The Tonight Show?*"

You should do it. And there are quite a number of reasons why.

The Tonight Show is a good example of several things.

In the first place it is an illustration of the three principal things that can happen when people communicate with others. They can (1) inform, (2) persuade, and (3) entertain.

People who go on *The Tonight Show* are usually trying to

People on The Tonight Show *look terrific.*

do a combination of at least two of these things, if not all three. People are there to dance, sing songs, tell jokes, talk about books, plug new records or movies, and let the audience know about upcoming appearances in night clubs or theaters.

Several other good things are happening in the experience. Can you guess what they are?

When people appear on a nationally televised talk show such as *The Tonight Show*:

1. They have a clear-cut reason or objective for appearing.

2. They are usually competent at what they do.

3. They are carefully prepared in briefings or rehearsals before they go on.

4. They operate within well-defined limits of time.

5. They look as good as possible (because of makeup, costumes, good lighting, and nice sets).

6. The audience is predisposed to be interested in what the speaker or performer is going to say or do.

7. There is a large staff of helpers to make things go smoothly and easily beforehand.

8. They have the confidence of knowing that they are on the set with one or more seasoned, talented performers whom they can lean on if they need to.

Since none of these things is usually the case when you are asked to get up there and talk, you shouldn't get up there and talk.

Generally, conditions are precisely the opposite. In other words:

1. Your reasons for appearing are often vague.

2. You may or may not be competent at what you're trying to do.

3. There is minimal preparation and *no* rehearsal.

4. There are no particular time limits.

5. Nobody looks good under fluorescent lights.

6. The audience usually doesn't know or care about you.

7. There isn't anybody to help you get ready.

8. There isn't anybody up there with you when you do it.

Few people fail on *The Tonight Show*. Few people succeed at the podium.

So the advice "Never speak to another audience again— *ever!*" is the safest, least tiring, and most successful path of all. If you chose to ignore this advice, your chances of failing are really quite astronomical.

I've arrived at this conclusion in two separate ways: one

extremely subjective and the other, I think, wholly objective.

Subjectively speaking, I have seen great numbers of people attempt to speak in front of groups, but very few have succeeded; very few combined attractive appearance, good speaking voice, ease in front of an audience, and interesting content. Part of the reason is cultural. Americans seem to be a cocksure, bust-ahead kind of people who presume that because they read newspspers and talk on the telephone they are communication experts. They are famous at trying to "Wing It," and this seldom works in front of an audience.

But, that aside, there is some compelling objective evidence.

I mentioned earlier that people on talk shows have a lot going for them in terms of visual effects, colored lights, nice settings, costumes, makeup, music, careful rehearsals, and other kinds of support.

You have *none* of these things.

It's too bad, because our society has become very sophisticated at *watching* things. People in this country are accustomed to looking at wide-screen movies, color television, plays, nightclub acts, posters, colorful sports, magazines, neon signs, billboards, and all kinds of clever advertising. The most skillful communicators in the world try to get through to us daily.

This represents the competition! In other words, when *you* stand up there in front of a group and serve as the focus of attention, you are unconsciously (or consciously) compared with these other media. Your come off very poorly by comparison. There is nothing magical about you.

So get out.

Don't speak to groups.

If you have enough rank in your organization, simply announce that as a matter of policy you will no longer make presentations to anybody. About anything.

If you have less rank or status, you can say that you read in a respected business review (or *Cosmopolitan*) that people just don't *do* that any more.

Failing that, prevaricate. But take care and always stick to surefire American issues and blame your inability to speak that day on something connected with an obscure religious holiday, the Red Cross, the health of a pet, or the birthday party of somebody who is extremely old.

If none of *these* works out, you may have to resort to the mouth ploy. In this exercise you must avoid talking to people for a few days. If you *must* talk to somebody, cover your mouth with both hands and mumble a lot. Somewhere in the mumbling mention the following two facts: "Dentist said it was a damned close call" and "Gotta go easy on my mouth for a while." This will not only get you out of speaking, but you may actually be shunned by everyone for several weeks.

An alternative to getting out is to find somebody else to make the speech *for* you. This is really a great idea, particularly if you can find somebody who is good at it, who will devote the time to it, and who will make a point of understanding the information you want to communicate.

The only problem with this idea is that such a person might become little more than a narrator, and wouldn't be able to deal with questions as they came up. But you can handle this somehow. It may be that you can rely on such a person for a formal presentation of facts, leaving you with a less formal, more comfortable question-and-answer period or discussion in a more relaxed atmosphere.

Chances are, though, that you're too unsure of yourself

to delegate this responsibility, even though it would limit *your* exposure to the audience to something as safe and simple as, "Thank you all for joining us. I want to begin by reviewing all the aspects of the current problem. I've asked Ed Nordness to handle this end of it, and he's done a comprehensive job. Eddie, go ahead."

(It's too bad that serious consideration can't be given to this suggestion. Hundreds of thousands of people in this country have been *trained* to speak other people's words believably. Every year, hundreds of men and women graduate from universities with degrees in theater, speech, and radio/television broadcasting. Only a microscopic part of 1 percent ever make it to Broadway or Los Angeles. The rest are out there percolating through the countryside, selling insurance or encyclopedias, and just waiting for a company or an organization to run an ad reading: "WANTED—*Retread actor or announcer to talk with mouth for pay. Must look OK, sound convincing, and know what to do with hands. No other experience required.*")

I don't know; that may be too radical an idea.

But here's something even *more* outrageous! Since I'm pretty sure you won't try to avoid speeches or delegate the responsibility *for* them, I'm going to suggest you find a *critic*.

I'd like you to walk up to a subordinate or an associate and say the following:

"Look, Gene, I want you to do something. I'm making a talk today and I want you to watch it and then talk to me about it afterward. I want you to be honest with me and tell me if I'm doing anything wrong. If I'm picking my nose, or not talking loud enough, or not making any sense, I want you to tell me about it. I want you to see if my facts are clear, or if I even *say* anything. And don't pull any punches.

Will you do that, Gene? And not just come up to me later and say, 'Terrific job!'?"

Would you do that?

Probably not, because you might get your feelings hurt.

The people who need this kind of help the most are the least likely to ask for it. They include a wide range of fairly competent (but boring) experts, bureaucrats, and most members of pressure groups. People such as these invariably think that the merit of their ideas, the righteousness of their cause, or the justice of their position will carry the day—and certainly more than offset any defects in presentation.

Well, I'm afraid this isn't so.

The way information is packaged and delivered is of paramount importance. It is essential that speakers be articulate, project well as people, and put an audience at ease. Once these qualifications are met, there can be some concentration on the *message*.

This country has never paid much attention to wild-eyed, incoherent loudmouths. We have vested the real power in people who appear (in public at least) to be calm, considerate, and thoughtful people. They look good. They're even-tempered yet forceful. They project the feeling that they are capable. This may be the first step in getting elected, or appointed to a position of responsibility.

2. If You Won't Quit, at Least Go Someplace Else or Do Something Different

I've seen a lot of grim conference rooms in this country. And a lot of dismal meeting places. A good many of them have no windows. Most of them are lit with fluorescent lights.

Cool white fluorescent light represents one of the great backward leaps of civilization (second only to office copiers, which put everybody in the publishing business and contribute to the wide-scale proliferation and circulation of garbage). People look like hell under cool white fluorescent lights. They seem too blue and too harsh.

And that's only the light. Most offices and meeting places in schools, businesses, and government facilities are dull, sterile, and deadly. "Office" furniture usually means awful furniture. Battleship gray still hangs on in a lot of places, and, while it may not look too bad on a cruiser or an aircraft carrier, it's the worst color anybody could pick for a desk, a file cabinet, or the tile on a floor.

Meetings are usually held in the worst places imaginable—in gray little rooms, in funny little auditoriums with fixed seating, or in "conference" rooms containing too much dark wood paneling and enormous tables that serve more to isolate people than to facilitate easy communication. I will complain more about this in Chapter 12.

Try not to get stuck with things like that. If you're really determined to talk to a group of people, find an unusual, but suitable, place to do it. Use your imagination.

In the meantime, let me remind you of something you already know about. When did you last have a business lunch with somebody? Or *any* kind of a lunch? Within the last week? Within the last month?

What do you remember about that meeting? Who was trying to do what to whom? Were you trying to persuade somebody to do something? Were they trying to persuade you?

Did anybody succeed?

Chances are pretty good that some business got done, ideas got exchanged, or something pleasant happened.

Restaurants are marvelous places to make little presentations and make other people feel comfortable. If you take somebody to a restaurant, some benefits automatically accrue to you. Going to a restaurant is something you have to arrange for (and therefore think about) ahead of time. If you have picked a good restaurant, the stage setting will be good. You will find plenty of props to work with (knives, forks, salt and pepper shakers, swizzle sticks, and so forth). Chances are you will have good lighting. People look terrific in a good restaurant because a lot of care has been taken with the lights. People also know they look like hell if they have to sit in a pool of green or blue light. (These colors don't do a whole lot for food either, except make it look as if it's been sitting outdoors for a long time.) Finally, the "audience" knows it will benefit from the lunch, if not from some business, social, or political standpoint, then at least from getting a drink and something good to eat.

The audience's level of expectation going into a restaurant is altogether different from what it is when you lead them into a stinky gym full of metal folding chairs.

You can more easily make people comfortable in a good restaurant. And once they're comfortable, they are much more disposed to listen to what you have to say.

This theory holds true for the greatest number of personal relationships. Not too many interesting propositions are developed, or accepted, under cool white fluorescent lights.

The only problem with a restaurant is that you can talk to only a limited number of people. Any more than six at a table makes successful communication difficult. (Much can be said for keeping groups as small as possible. The more people in a meeting, the greater the chance of confusion and misunderstanding—or, worse yet, anger, fear, and other bad things.)

When you *do* have more people, you've simply got to go someplace else, or do something different. Following are a few ideas.

Private dining rooms in restaurants or private clubs are great, particularly if you can depend on quality service. This is also true of suites in good hotels. You can deal with a larger number of people (such as eight to twelve) with ease. You can have blackboards or easel pads on hand and create informal, shirt-sleeves–atmosphere presentations. You can open a small bar when you feel like it, and serve hors d'oeuvres or a meal.

I've been to meetings in penthouses and they were sensational. So are meetings aboard ships or boats. (They don't even have to *go* anyplace, but can remain tied to a pier.) Trains would be fun if we had any, and I've heard of meetings on buses and planes. Lodges, resorts, and motels are naturals, of course.

You can also throw a picnic or relate the meeting to some time-honored activity such as fishing, hunting, gambling, or hanging around the center of a big city where there's lots of shopping.

I've always wanted to reserve the Goodyear blimp for a small meeting some time. I would serve some nice food and fly along the coast somewhere. People would remember that meeting for a hundred years.

Give it some thought.

Let me conclude this section about doing something different by making a suggestion about television. In a lot of companies these days are some simple little television recorders. Here's what I'd like you to try: Find somebody who can set up a camera for you and then teach you how to turn the machine on and off (and how to rewind it so you can play it back).

Then you can do a little television all by yourself.

You can open a small bar if you feel like it.
Do anything you can to succeed.

Fix it so that you stand in the picture with everything showing from your knees upward, then turn everything on and go up there for three or four minutes and talk about your job (or something else you know about). Be sure to turn the monitor around so you can't see yourself while you're recording.

Play it back and look carefully at what you did.

It will be disconcerting at first if you've never heard your own voice before. You will probably sound like Charlotte Zimmermann or Pierce Burford, but don't worry about that.

Look at your hands.

Look at your body.

Look at your eyes.

Listen to the *content* of what you're saying.

Discover how convincing or persuasive you sound.

Try it several times, and remember that this is exactly what an audience sees and hears.

Seeing yourself on television may be a little disconcerting at first.

3. The Author's Early Career with His Mouth, etc.

Let me take a few minutes and talk about *my* particular mouth.

I don't know why I started appearing in front of audiences in the first place. As nearly as I can remember, the process has always frightened me to death.

One of the earliest recollections is standing in a woodshed in a small Oregon town trying to memorize the lines for a pageant. I remember looking at the sky and saying aloud, "If I ever get through this one, I'll never do it again." That night I was moderately successful in three speaking parts (and three costume changes), as a black cat, a brownie, and the minute hand of a clock.

From that point forward I persisted in the idea that it was somehow an all right thing to do, because it entertained people, or it entertained me, or something. This led to a shaky, on-off, and finally abortive attempt at being an actor—an exercise that took the better part of eight years. In a couple of colleges, I worked in shoe-box theaters, children's theaters, tents, theaters-in-the-round, and basements. I worked in summer-stock companies, in companies that moved by truck, and in companies that moved by airplane. In the service I ran a small radio station, and later I worked as a comedian in loud, drunk little West Coast nightclubs. Toward the end I did live television in Denver—as a small-time sheriff on a children's show and as a hillbilly on a Western variety show. All told, I think I earned about $181.

Although I made little money, I learned a few things from the experience. Let me tell you about them.

The main thing is this: Even with speakers or entertainers who are *used* to being in front of people, things can always go seriously wrong. Sets fall down, lights explode, and zippers unzip. People get overconfident. Or they get so wound up in what they're doing they forget about the audience.

One of the valuable things I got from theatrical training embarrassed me at first. But I got over it. Among the classes an actor has to take is a cross between calisthenics and ballet. The yearlong course I took was called Rhythmic and Dramatic Movement. It sounds very sweet, but it was difficult as hell. The net effect of all the miserable exercises and the arm and leg waving was that we could thenceforth walk across a stage with a fair chance of not falling over the furniture or knocking down a set. We could move around on the stage and look fairly natural. It began to answer the question "What do I do with my hands (or my arms, legs, feet, and body)?"

Another thing about theater was learning about long rehearsals.

And I also learned that the process of looking good on a

stage is a very complicated business and altogether artificial. Somebody (and a staff) has to worry a great deal about the background setting you work against. Somebody else, with another staff, worries about costumes that will work for you, for the play, and *with* the setting. The right props have to be found. Makeup has to be planned and applied properly. Lighting has to be developed with the needs of the play in mind, but also in consideration of the sets, the costumes, and the makeup. The actors have to rehearse, not only to remember lines, but to be able to speak them as though they were being spoken for the first time. The director is at the top of everything and controls it all—the people onstage and off, the appearance of everything, and the needs of the play in terms of the content, continuity, and pace of the material.

Even when *all* these aspects are carefully coordinated and executed by professionals, shows can still fail. They simply fail to work.

Now, compare *that* sort of careful effort to your own attempts at being a speaker in front of a group. It's the same thing as *The Tonight Show* I mentioned earlier.

Chances are you haven't rehearsed. You have no specialized lighting. There is little concern for costumes or how you will look. You very often have little concern for the audience and what they want or need—and little, if any, information about what it's going to be like up there in front of them.

But most all of us, in our daydreams, are spellbinders. Courtroom defense attorneys. Speakers who can mesmerize any audience. These daydreams are often so real that we make remarks like, "Things will be OK. I'll just get up there and . . . uh. . . ."

(You remember, don't you? Wing It!)

When the chips are finally down, however, the story is quite different. We're all alone. We don't really know what we're doing. Our armpits are soaked, our stomachs don't feel so good, and our knees tremble. We still have a shred of confidence left, though.

We pin all our hopes on our mouth.

And then it opens. A thin, reedy, Donald Duck voice comes out. Or a coughing fit. Or a string of "um's" and "uh's" so prolonged that people begin to wonder if you're trying to do the whole thing in Morse code.

It's a million laughs.

In our daydreams we're all terrific speakers. So we think we can Wing It. Then the big moment comes and we open our mouths. . . . You know the rest.

4.Trying to Help Others with Their Mouths (Another Short Career)

After the experience with theater and live television (and shots at such career opportunities as fry cook, shrubbery salesman, bellhop, and teletype operator), I infiltrated U.S. industry and became an industrial film producer. One of the things that seemed very reasonable about motion pictures was that if you ever succeeded in doing something right, you would have a permanent record of it. You could also exercise some control over the content of the material, the way in which the content was strung together, and the speed with which the information was presented. (Those, by the way, are the components of *your* next speech: content, continuity, and pace.)

I discovered that while this is theoretically true, there are pitfalls, mechanical and otherwise. Some of them have to do with weather and the statistical improbabilities of going seventeen days with no sunshine. Other problems arise when you load film magazines backward, forget to bring the battery for the camera motor, or drop the entire camera out of an airplane. One of the biggest thrills, however, is to successfully accomplish all the photography and then get a call from the laboratory telling you that something incredible has happened. Such as a "slight scratch" on "part" of the film which translates eventually as a ¼-inch gouge down the center of 2,700 feet of original. I remember one conversation that began: "Listen, I know how fantastic this is going to sound to you . . . the idea that a film processor could catch *fire*. . . ."

But all those details aside, the biggest single problem of film is the same as that of a face-to-face meeting with a group—too many words and too much detail.

I then got involved in advertising and promotion. I saw this as the ultimate communications challenge—using short bursts of words and pictures, and influencing people by getting immediately to the point.

During this period I spent an interlude in New York, doing presentations for advertising agencies and other clients. In many cases we were involved in the design, development, and production of an entire presentation. Sometimes we produced only visuals.

It came as a big surprise to me to learn that New York advertising agencies (supposedly the slickest communicators anywhere) were capable of mounting spectacularly dull presentations. The main reason for failure was one of the most common worldwide—too many people simultaneously trying to be in charge.

Let me tell you about some purely *mechanical* problems.

In one classic instance all I had to do was "take care of the little details for somebody doing a twenty-minute presentation at the Plaza Hotel." I would like to describe this event in detail, because it illustrates a few of the problems that come up when you make an all-out effort to produce something that is supposed to look easy, comfortable, and relaxed.

The client was interested in showing a large group of tourist agency people some information about an area of the Mediterranean. The audience was already assembled for a convention, so it was decided that a buffet breakfast and a short presentation would be easiest to handle. The client cheerfully added that I could use their projector. That conversation took place on Wednesday afternoon. The presentation was scheduled for Friday morning.

Arrangements had been made to use the grand ballroom of the Plaza because the expected audience would number two or three hundred. I looked at the room and discovered that the distance from the screen to an alcove where I could stick a projector was about 80 feet. At such a distance it is no longer possible to use unmodified home projectors.

I also discovered that it was more than simply a matter of *one* projector. In addition to 35mm slides, there was also a portion of a filmstrip, and some TV commercials on 16mm film. Doing the job successfully required the use of four projectors, and four uncommon projectors at that. They would need special light sources to project a bright picture over such a long distance.

Thursday morning I was on hand with two Plaza Hotel electricians and a consulting engineer from a New York audiovisual equipment rental company.

It was simple. We needed two Carousel projectors with custom-made xenon light sources and a heavy-duty dissolve unit to go back and forth between the two 35mm projectors. We needed a 16mm projector with a xenon light source. And we needed a filmstrip projector with a xenon light

Sometimes it isn't a matter of just one projector.

source. Each projector, regardless of format, required a lens of a certain focal length in order to fill the screen. When we found the right lenses, we discovered that the Plaza's screen wasn't quite the right size for our purposes, and so we brought in another one. A bigger one.

The 16mm film had a sound track, the output of which had to go into a special amplifier. The amplifier needed was different from that required by the Plaza's sound system; that meant we had to get a completely separate one, including different speakers.

So we put a couple of speakers on the stage and ran their cables back to the amplifier for 80 feet. The 16mm projector worked like a champ.

The filmstrip projector (which plays an LP record) didn't

work like a champ. It didn't work at all. The engineer called in an assistant.

I, meanwhile, investigated the problem of the client's using the Plaza's microphone and PA system in conjunction with *our* sound system, but ours caused a feedback problem. (Microphone feedback is that wonderful dying-pig noise.)

We decided, therefore, to have the speaker's microphone go through our own sound system. That would simplify things. So we found a compatible microphone and ran its mike cable the 80 feet back to the amplifier. (This process, called learning-as-you-go-along, necessitated numerous urgent calls to the equipment rental company for some new items to be delivered. They were thrilled.)

Five P.M. came. The filmstrip sound system problem was solved, but the speaker's microphone developed a loud buzz. The alcove in the back of the ballroom was starting to fill up with cables.

A friend dropped in and foolishly asked if he could help. I said, "Sure." I think he might have meant to stay for fifteen minutes. He was there until midnight and returned for two hours the following day.

At about 6 P.M. it occurred to somebody that the speaker was supposed to advance the 35mm slides as he narrated them. This happens all the time, so remote cables are made for Carousel projectors. It works out, however, that very few 90-foot remote cables are around at any given moment.

A man was dispatched to find one or build one. We simultaneously cured the microphone buzz, but developed a hum in the 16mm projector.

Evening, as they say, fell on Gotham.

We began to address the problem (the simple problem) of the compound movement that takes place when you (1) bring down the house lights and (2) bring up the stage lights. This isn't a particularly difficult thing to do, and it looks nice. Much better than cutting house lights (and being plunged in darkness) and then snapping on the stage lights. This is too abrupt and painful. You want the house lights to dim gradually, and simultaneously have stage lights appear on the speaker (actor, talent, or whatever you want to call him). The audience are then able to shift their attention very easily from the room and the crowd to the person on the stage. As the lights dim, the audience prepares to listen and watch.

We faced only two small problems at the Plaza. The dimmers were at the other end of the room from us, and the lights weren't set up yet.

By 11 P.M. all the necessary electrical work had been traced, checked, fixed, and tested. We had eliminated the last of the hums, buzzes, shrieks, and clicks. The lights worked.

By way of a final rehearsal we tested everything in the order it was supposed to be used. The 16mm film broke.

It is easy to splice 16mm film. All you need is a splicer and some film cement. Plaza room service can do a lot of marvelous things, but they can't be expected to provide 16mm film splicers. I called anyway.

The equipment company had splicers. The engineer worked for the equipment company, but he didn't have his key. So he called somebody who did. As these events unfolded I missed the last train to Chappaqua.

The splicer arrived and my friend decided to leave. With him went the engineer, the engineer's assistant, and two electricians. They all promised to return in the morning.

As I examined the break in the film I saw that it had failed at a splice. Since the film was a collection of television commercials glued end to end I decided to take a look at all the other splices. They seemed weak so I respliced all of them.

At about 2 P.M. I was checking the 35mm slides when a lamp burned out. But that's easy. The engineer had worried about that and there were plenty of spares. Figuring out how to replace the bulb (or even find the bulb) was another matter, but I finally managed.

I then decided that one of the slides was dirty, so I took it out to clean it. I dropped it. (If you're clever, you mount 35mm transparencies between two pieces of glass. That way you keep the film clean. If the glass gets dusty you can very easily wipe off the glass. Also, the focus of the projector is simpler because all the slides ride in the same position when projected.) When I dropped the slide I broke one of the pieces of the cover glass.

This time I didn't bother room service with a request for 2- by 2-inch cover glass. Instead I walked a few blocks across town to our shop and got the material. On the way a hooker asked me if I couldn't think of anything better to do than whatever it was that I was doing. Later on I thought of some remarkably funny things I could have said.

I returned and fixed the slide.

I then noticed that the chairs were arranged funny. So I fooled around with them for a while.

At about 4 A.M. I walked uptown to my boss's apartment. He was out of town. I gave some thought to why it was that Good Old Herb was in San Francisco (where it was only 1 A.M.) having a good time, while I was in New York having a nervous breakdown over something that seemed so trivial.

I stared at the ceiling and estimated the number of things that could go wrong later that day. I quit when I got to about fifty-three.

The next morning everybody showed up early for a run-through. We worked out a flashlight signaling system to communicate with the electrician on the dimmers at the other end of the room.

The man who was going to narrate the presentation arrived and was doing fine until I mistakenly showed him the setup in the back of the room. He began waving his arms and saying that it was too complicated—far too complicated.

I felt like screaming, "I agree! I agree!" but instead calmly convinced him that everything would be just fine. We made a successful run-through (during which I noticed that the lectern light would shine in the eyes of the audience, and quickly masked it off).

A few minutes later the audience came in and took their seats. The house lights went down very smoothly, and the lights on the speaker came up full. When he spoke, the volume was at just the right level, with the proper amount of treble and bass. He proceeded easily and introduced the first of the 35mm slides. The lights dimmed on the speaker, and the first projector gradually came to its full brightness.

The slide show progressed, and as the last slide dimmed on the screen, the spotlights eased back on the speaker. He then introduced the previous year's filmstrip, and we cut to a point in the middle of it. This meant turning on the projector, putting the needle down at the right point on the record, and bringing the sound up slowly. It worked. The sequence ended where it was supposed to end. The projector went off and the lights went back up for the speaker to introduce the TV commercials. The film ran through without breaking, and the sound level was correct.

At the end of the film, the projector faded to black, and the lights went back on the speaker for his brief concluding remarks. He finished, the spotlights dimmed, the audience applauded, and the house lights went back up.

Everything had gone smoothly. The audience had been able to hear and see everything with ease. The talk was compact and interesting, enriched with a great deal of visual material.

The audience went back to the buffet and were ready for another easy day.

They left behind a half-dozen people, at least four of whom were drenched with sweat, from both the heat of the equipment and the strain of trying to do things right.

This simple, easy little presentation took just over eighteen minutes, but required about eighteen pieces of gear, several hundred feet of cable, and dozens of worker-hours. We spent four hours just breaking things down and putting them back in boxes. It was expensive, in terms of worker-hours and equipment rental, but the result was well worth the cost to the client.

From this experience I was able to deduce several things. The first I had already known: audiovisual equipment isn't really portable and shouldn't be moved around very much—it works best if it's installed and left alone. Also, once you get an installation rigged and wired it will be "right" from that point onward with a minimum of maintenance and tweaking of knobs. You should have no further worry about microphones, lenses, or any of the rest of it. In short—make permanent installations.

Another important conclusion was that if you decide to go for broke and do a big, smooth, theatrical number, be sure to allow a little bit of time to do it. Haste makes disasters.

The final conclusion was the simplest. I decided I was too old and too nervous for that line of work.

5. Why *I* Got Out of Show Business

I'm sure everyone has heard the story about the guy who smells awful all the time. When asked the reason for this he explains that it's because of his job—working in a circus giving enemas to elephants. The listener asks, "Why don't you get another job?" and the guy replies hotly, "What! And get out of *show business?*"

I was more than ready to get out, particularly if show business meant standing in the back of the Plaza ballroom with my shirt sticking to me. (As things worked out, I needn't have worried. I was caught in an ad agency purge a few weeks later and fired.)

I gravitated to a large firm where my charter was to wander around and try to help people make better presentations. In the process of doing this (without any particular success) I was asked by my boss to help with the development of a comprehensive course called Unified Communications. It had been asked for by a government agency, and the subject matter was to include writing, listening, interviewing, group dynamics, reading, and speaking. Would I handle the speaking part and write down everything I knew about the subject?

I said that I would.

I went home and wrote about half a page. "Bill," I said the next day, "I have some bad news. Now that I *think* about it, I don't *know* anything about the process of speaking to groups. I just seem to know when people are doing it wrong." Bill smiled very slightly and changed the subject to how it is to be out of work.

His observations inspired me to write about twenty pages which, he correctly noted, were devoid of any sense of organization. After several more false starts, I developed a

Things did not go flawlessly for me
in Washington, D.C.

series of lectures. The whole idea frightened me pretty badly, simply because it seemed foolhardy to speak to a group on the subject of speaking to groups. Such a presentation must be flawless if the presenter is to be credible.

Flawless it wasn't, and I was incredible. When we opened in Washington, D.C., I speared myself with a pointer, tripped over microphone cables, spilled my notes on the floor, got completely lost a time or two, and messed up generally.

In the course of doing these lectures elsewhere, I ran into somebody who knew what he was doing. He advised me to let the audience get more involved—give *them* things to do. This, he said, would be good for two reasons. They would have more to keep themselves occupied, and I wouldn't have to talk so much (thus decreasing the likelihood of my messing up any further).

After that time I began each discussion by dividing the audience into groups of two and asking them what *their* problems were as *speakers*. They were asked to talk about these problems for a while and make a list. Then, each group would decide on a representative to report to the entire group. This technique involved everybody and made speakers out of half of them.

Following these brief presentations, I would ask the same groups of two to put together a list of the most serious problems that an *audience* has. Then the other person on the team would stand before the group and discuss the list.

At the end of the session, we would have a great many things to talk about, and, by that time, of course, each person in the group would have participated actively as a speaker.

I have done this with many groups of people. They have ranged from middle and top management people, business school graduates, foreign students, and homemakers in typical suburban neighborhoods. The results are always surprisingly the same. Everybody mentions about the same things. The typical list looks something like this.

People who have to *speak* say:

1. I get stage fright.
2. I have trouble getting, and keeping, attention.
3. I don't have enough self-confidence.
4. I don't know my material well enough to do it easily.
5. I have trouble getting the information together.
6. I don't know what to do with my hands.
7. I have trouble keeping to the allotted time.
8. I don't know how to handle the discussion that *follows* a presentation.
9. I have trouble keeping my *own* interest up.
10. I have trouble organizing information for a presentation.

People who have to *listen* say:

1. The speaker was dull, boring, and monotonous.
2. It was very confusing because the speaker wasn't well organized.
3. It was too *long*.
4. The speaker had no convictions about the subject.
5. We couldn't *hear* the speaker.
6. The speaker talked too fast.
7. We were in a bad place. There were too many distractions.
8. The speaker had strange mannerisms.
9. The speaker had no personality.
10. There wasn't anything in it for *me*.

Many other complaints have been made, but these are the common ones, so we'll look at them in greater detail in Chapters 6 and 7.

But, before we go any further, we're going to have a little snap quiz. It's about the introduction to this book.

Remember the introduction?

Here are some questions:

1. How many rings are there in the symbol of the Olympic Games?

2. What colors are they?

3. What do the colors mean?

4. Where did I hear the advice about the chewing gum? (On television? In an impromptu talk? Where?)

5. Did a woman or a man tell me about it?

6. What material do you use to get gum out of your hair?

7. What were the illustrations about one part per million? One inch in how many miles? One minute in how many years?

8. How do you stop a charging lion?

Very good.

I'd be willing to bet a hundred dollars that you got most of these questions right.

I then concluded the introduction by listing five things that are important to a talk. Do you remember what the five things were?

I'd be willing to bet a *thousand* dollars that you can't get three out of five. (If you can't remember, it isn't because you're stupid, but because it is difficult to remember certain concepts and principles. So please review that list in the Introduction. You might also be interested in consulting the last item in Checklist A.

If you want to, we can continue now. (I've tried to talk you out of it, but if you *have* to get up there and speak, I think the following may be of some help.)

We'll start with *your* problems.

6. Problems You Say *You* Have

Let's begin with a discussion of some of the problems *you* think you have. I keep hearing things like:

1. *"I get stage fright."*

Well, so do I. Everybody gets stage fright to some extent. A few people only get nervous. Others get physically sick. One of the first things to remember is to be quiet about it. Most of the time nervousness doesn't show a bit, and if you don't say anything about it, nobody will know the difference. If you mention the fact (or apologize for any other shortcoming in delivery or content), you make the audience very sensitive to it. As they become sensitive to it, *they* get nervous and can't concentrate. They are distracted and can't hear the information you really want them to hear.

Stage fright is a combination of a lot of things, but mainly a function of (1) the place, (2) the audience, and (3) your own material.

You can do something about the first by becoming familiar with the place in which you will speak. If you will be speaking from a stage, you've got to get on it ahead of time. Walk around on it, find the lectern, see where the microphone cables are located and where you operate any necessary projector controls. Find out how to enter and exit comfortably. If there are stairs down to the audience area, walk down them. Step into the audience area and sit down in a few different seats. Try to understand the view the audience will have of you. Wander around the place for a few minutes. Get familiar with it.

Many readers will now complain, "There isn't *time* to do that. Sometimes I don't even *know* where the meeting is going to be. They sometimes don't decide until the last minute."

You are merely covering up for laziness.

Simply tell people that, unless you are informed well ahead of time what the facilities are going to be like (and given ample opportunity to inspect them), you won't cooperate. The deal's off. But *you* have to make a point of it. Nobody else will.

If you must persist in appearing before audiences, you can also do other things to eliminate stage fright. Get plenty of experience, anyplace you can get it. Speak to service organizations. Teach a Sunday School class. Take an evening class in public speaking, or try out for a play. A smart thing would be teaching a class within your own organization, one that meets one evening a week for a few weeks.

A second major cause of stage fright is, of course, the audience. It seems to me that the more you know about them, the easier it is to appear (although I know some speakers who find it almost impossible to stand up in front of people they've known for years).

By and large, however, meeting some of the audience ahead of time will help. Failing that, you can certainly discharge some of your responsibility to acquaint the audience ahead of time with who *you* are, what you're trying to do, what they're expected to do, and how long they're expected to sit there. I'll talk more about that later.

Finally, your own material may be driving you crazy. If you're really not sure of your facts, or the order in which the facts will be presented, you have every right to be terrified.

2. *"I have trouble getting, and keeping, attention."*

The answer to this is fairly simple. If you're talking to the same audiences over and over again, you've probably set a bad pattern. People have a low level of expectation about you that is usually fulfilled.

Your trouble is that you give rotten speeches. They are probably confusing and overly long. Keeping the attention of an audience depends on a whole lot of things, many of which are listed at the end of this book.

You really need the person I told you about—somebody to tell you quite honestly what he or she thinks. I've developed a special form to help do that. It is also at the end of the book.

The best advice: be brief.

3. *"I don't have enough self-confidence."*

Don't worry about it right now.

4. *"I don't know my material well enough to do it easily."*

Learn it. I don't like to be abrupt with you, but there are some things you simply can't fake. Obviously, this piece of advice isn't meant to suggest that you learn everything in the world about your subject. You can't do that. There isn't time. Also, there wouldn't be time for you to play it all back to an audience. Know the material you *have* chosen for an audience—the facts you've decided are relevant.

5. *"I have trouble getting my information together."*

I know that. It's a real problem. But you know what? The real issue is that we usually get too *much* information together and don't know what to do with it. We don't know which parts to present and which to set aside. We also get very introspective and forget what the audience *wants* to know or *needs* to know. I think you will be helped with this problem when we talk about audiences.

6. *"I don't know what to do with my hands."*

Well, what have you ever *tried* to do with your hands? Anything? You don't just all of a sudden start knowing what to do with your hands. They're a real problem. Here are a few ideas.

If you're really a hopeless case, carry a small stack of 3- by 5- or 5- by 8-inch cards in one hand and carry them at your side at about your waistline. That hand will then be safe, and you won't have to worry about it.

Now for the other hand. Put a pencil in it. You can then wave the pencil around a little bit (or, once in a while, hold up the cards and appear to mark them with the pencil—thus making you look very thorough). You can also hold a pipe or a pair of glasses in your right hand. For *rapt* attention, you might try holding a revolver.

To really solve the problem, you must *exercise*, and do stuff with your hands that you don't normally do. You've got to stop making those halfhearted little gestures in which the hands always hover in an area somewhere between the hips and the belly button.

Get those babies up in the air! Shoot them straight out from the shoulder, first to the left and then to the right. Point your index finger straight out in front of you. Stick both arms up in the air in a big V. Every time you get near a mirror, point at yourself (with a gesture that's kept above the sternum) and shout, "*Hey*, baby!" or "Thattaway to go!" This may startle a few people in the rest room, but don't worry about it.

For another good exercise, try imitating trapeze artists as they give their bows at the end of their act. That's a position in which both arms are fully extended, slightly above the shoulders, with the arms slightly bent at the elbows and the hands outstretched. Chest well out. You can then slowly turn from the left to the right, as though to a whole big circus tent full of people. It's a little tough to work into a presentation, but it's terrific when you finally do.

Be a baseball umpire. Be an eagle.

You can also do some fake swordplay with a yardstick, or, almost as good, conduct an orchestra with a ruler. Get in there and put those arms in some positions they don't usually get into. Exercise! *Wave them around!* Pretty soon they'll start doing a few things by themselves.

(I'll tell you what. Put the book down right now, wherever you are. Now make the gesture a baseball umpire makes for *Out!* Or, better yet, the signal for *Safe!* If anybody looks at you strangely, tell them you're in rehearsal for a play about eagles.)

If you can't use any of *this* advice, then consult Checklist L.

7. *"I have trouble keeping to the allotted time."*

Keep to the allotted time (as defined by you or somebody else), or, better yet, *under* it. Or risk boring everybody to death. It's your choice. Knowing what you're talking about gives you a big advantage in dealing with the problem. One of the greatest rewards you can get from an audience is gratitude (via smiles, applause, and congratulations) when you successfully reduce one of your traditional fifty-minute ramblings to a tight and lucid ten-minute presentation.

8. *"I don't know how to handle the discussion that follows a presentation."*

Several things must happen in order to solve this problem to the satisfaction of the audience. You have to establish two-way communication, pave the way for some action to take place, invite (and get) participation, and, finally, be responsible for the eventual outcome of the things jointly discussed. It isn't reasonable for you to ask for good ideas, get them, and then promptly ignore them. Ideas must be accepted or rejected for adequate and understandable reasons.

One technique that works is getting statements or questions from the audience and writing them on a blackboard or on large sheets of paper that can then be hung up around the room. The audience then sees its own input and can begin to discuss ways of dealing with it.

If the input is great, chances are it can't be sufficiently discussed in one meeting, and another should be scheduled. You may need to ask for volunteers to follow through, or to make some assignments to specific individuals so that action will result and progress can be measured.

9. *"I have trouble keeping my own interest up."*

That's bad, because an audience can tell very easily if you have any real enthusiasm or excitement for your subject. If you're really not interested in what you're talking about, do as I'm doing. Get out of show business. Learn how to play the violin. Join VISTA. Leave the country. But do something else. Don't inflict your indifference on other people.

10. *"I have trouble organizing information."*

This is related to *collecting* information for a talk, and we'll discuss this later.

7. Problems the Audience Says *It* Has Because of You

1. *"The speaker was dull, boring, and monotonous."*

I mentioned before that I thought this applied to almost *all* speakers, because of who we are and the mythology we grew up on. Winging it is the tendency. Taking the easy way out is a lot more fun than thinking anything through. Additionally, speakers tend to be dull in direct proportion to their dull surroundings.

2. *"It was very confusing because the speaker wasn't well organized."*

This is also part of being dull and boring. Monotony is generated by people who undertake to tell *everything* they know about a subject. Organization takes some work and a real willingness to communicate useful information.

(I suppose that it's actually a good thing that people are as disorganized as they are. If everybody started communicating in a lucid, forthright way, the country would probably collapse. At least 68 percent of the work force would be recognized as superfluous.)

I wonder what really *would* happen if we started to communicate with each other with the same precision, clarity, and simplicity we use to communicate with a computer. A computer isn't very bright; it's merely very fast. Putting anything *in* a computer is a laborious, time-consuming, and very specialized process. A computer is fed little bits of information one at a time in a logical sequence. It isn't given a lot of irrelevant information. Also, you can't kid it along, you don't lie to it, and you can't influence it with emotion. Neither can you threaten it, fire it, or flatter it. The first time you try to cross a computer, it'll get you. Garbage in— garbage out. We can't apply this lesson in human relations, I suppose, because it's not part of the American heritage to show the same consideration for people that we show for machines.

3. *"It was too long."*

Same problem as above, with possibly an even greater indifference to the audience.

4. *"The speaker had no convictions about the subject."*

We've covered this subject adequately by suggesting that if *you* can't show any enthusiasm, then you can hardly expect such a reaction from an audience. Lack of conviction might be offset by extreme brevity. Speak quickly and sit down.

5. *"We couldn't hear the speaker."*

Among the simplest and most rudimentary standards to be met is the demand that the audience be able to *hear* and *see* the speaker. Incredibly enough, these obvious rules are broken daily. It is unprofessional, unbusinesslike, and totally unbelievable. Often it's a bureaucratic problem in which somebody of far greater rank is making a fool of himself or herself, but nobody has the nerve to say anything. Buy a copy of this book and mark this paragraph in red. The speaker will be pleased, not annoyed. Or maybe annoyed enough to change.

6. *"The speaker talked too fast."*

Slow down, even though you think it's killing you. You can cure this problem *only* with the help of somebody else—somebody who will listen to you and make an honest report on all the things you're doing. Read aloud slowly. Read against a clock. Read two minutes' worth, and then try to read the passage aloud again in two and a half minutes.

7. *"We were in the wrong place. Too many distractions."*

An all-too-common occurrence, this has happened to everybody—being in a room that was too small, too noisy, too cold, too hot, too stuffy, or had a large picture window overlooking something very interesting.

8. *"The speaker had strange mannerisms."*

If you put your hands in your pockets, or are apt to unconsciously scratch some place that itches, or pick your nose, this sort of thing can become a distraction so great that nobody will hear a word you say.

9. *"The speaker had no personality."*

Everybody has a personality. It's simply that most speakers make the worst of theirs.

10. *"There wasn't anything in it for me."*

There's an entire chapter in this book about the consideration you should give an audience. It's the *next* chapter.

8. What *about* the Audience?

The person best qualified (in terms of subject knowledge) to make a speech is often the worst person to *do* it. The specialist knows too much. The subject has become too much a part of his or her life. The person is more apt to think of the subject in terms of its own inherent value, rather than of its relationship to other facts, systems, organizations, or to people generally.

This person seldom deals with the question that every member of the audience asks: "What's in this for *me*? How do *I* benefit?"

They expect *something*.

Remember that your audience looks at you differently from the way they watch television or movies. In the latter case they anticipate pleasure. They hope to be entertained, and they are willing to invest their time (and money) in this anticipation. They hope for the best, seldom get it, and are not actively critical of what goes on.

People seldom anticipate pleasure, however, when they file into a conference room, meeting hall, or auditorium—and they are quite ready to be critical. They steel themselves for the experience. They are prepared to be confused and numbed by boredom. They know well ahead of time that meetings are usually a nuisance.

Later I will give you an idea of how to condition the audience *ahead* of your talk (Chapter 14), but right now let's take a look at the audience and some of their real needs and expectations.

Why don't *you* sit in the audience for a minute.

Now then, how can I get you to understand something?

(I am forced, of course, to rule out the six great all-time, surefire persuaders: the promise of food, sex, or wealth; and the threat of death, high levels of pain, or imprisonment. I do this with great reluctance because even a cursory glance at history shows their widespread use and great effectiveness.)

If I must rely on *facts* to change your mind, then here are a few of the things you might expect—or at least hope—that I would consider.

1. How much do you, and other members of the audience, already know about the subject?

2. How readily will you understand any specialized language (such as technical terms)?

3. How long have you had an interest in, or a connection with, the subject?

4. How concerned are you with the subject and its ramifications? (Unless I do a little investigating, I may gloss over a fact that is of paramount importance to you and the other members of the audience.)

5. How *opinionated* (as contrasted to informed) are you about the subject to be discussed? (I may also try to

gauge your opinion about *me*, the speaker, so that I will know ahead of time whether you will be apt to greet me with warmth, indifference, or out-and-out hostility. That kind of estimate should have a profound effect on both the subject matter and the manner of its delivery.)

6. How much help do you need to see the connection between what I'm *saying* and what you're *doing* (or living, thinking, or understanding)? The essential connection is often overlooked altogether.

7. Why did you attend? This is important to know. Often you attend because you have to, sometimes because you want to. If possible, it's important for me to precondition you to want to be there in the first place.

8. What's in it for *you?* I have to look very carefully to exploit the actual advantages that are going to accrue to you personally—the *benefits* of your listening to me and later behaving in some slightly (or markedly) different way. I must also be alert to the *disadvantages* that may be inherent in my presentation.

If I'm a really clever speaker, I will find some special relationship that exists between you and me, or between my organization (or company, church, civic or social group, or political party) and yours. And also find out about the length of that relationship.

I should also investigate all the past attempts at communicating with you and try to discover the ones that were most successful. (For example, I might discover that you would be more receptive to a talk that is informal and conversational than to one that is serious and highly technical.)

I should try to determine whether there is anything special about the situation (either for me or for you), such as the size of the audience, the time of day (or year), or the special nature of the occasion.

I should give thought to the words I will use and take a position about taboo words.

One must be very careful in deciding whether to use "obscene" language. In many cases you will find this not only acceptable and very useful, but desirable. (It is actually a further extension of one's ability to speak conversationally. Swearing is *very* conversational. It is also rich with subtlety and meaning. The old injunction against swearing as a "reflection of one's lack of vocabulary and imagination" is nonsense. If people feel comfortable with it, do it.)

I used to know somebody who would bring a very prim and proper person to every meeting to ensure that nobody would use strong language (and therefore say precisely what was on his or her mind). It forced us into lukewarm statements like, "Golly, we'd sure like to know what the heck's going on down there in the Southwestern Region," when something a whole lot stronger was clearly called for.

What is the stranger up there going to tell us?

A final problem for me to deal with is my *identity*. When an unknown person is suddenly presented to you, it's only natural to wonder, "Who is this person? Why is the person here? Where did the stranger come from? What can the stranger tell us that we don't know already?" This particular identity crisis should be taken care of early.

And I should consider *all* of the foregoing before I decide on the first two words of the speech.

You may now come back from the audience. It's time to get your thoughts together.

9. Getting Your Thoughts Together

A lot of interesting material has been written about how to determine the content of a speech, conduct research for the material, and organize the information. I haven't anything original to add to it, but I've put together the following questions to help you identify some of the loose ends.

Ask these standard, elementary questions when you begin to consider *any* kind of a story.

Who?

Who got us into this? Who warned us? Who lied to us? Who is a part of the problem? (We? They?) Who is in the case of important characters? Whom can we turn to for help? Who has further information? Who is in charge? Who should be hired? Who should be consulted? Whom shall we assign to work on this? Who is responsible? Who cares? Who has enough enthusiasm to do anything with this?

What?

What happened? In what sequence did it happen? What is *about* to happen? What are the conditions now? What were the conditions that led up to now? What are the events? What was the rationale? What was the plan? What are we going to do? What was the impact of the decision we made last year? What will be the outcome of our actions today? What the hell is going on?

Why?

Why did this happen? Why did this happen *now* (rather than sooner or later)? Why did this happen in exactly the *way* it happened? Why do we make the decisions we make? Why *us?* Why not *them?* Why did we do what we did? Why didn't we start doing it sooner? Why did we stop? Why don't we get organized? Why are we here?

Where?

Is this going on all over? Or just in Minneapolis? Where did it happen first? Where will it happen next? Where should *we* go? Where should we have gone last year? Where does it hurt us the most? Where can we get some relief? Where does it seem to be working? Where can we get some more of this good stuff?

When?

When did it happen? What time was it? What was the date? Is it continuing to happen *now?* If we'd been clever, when could we have seen this thing coming? When could we have done something? When did we really find out? When did we first suspect? When did we begin to react? When are we going to get started on *this* problem? When can we expect to see some progress? When are we going to make some assignments?

And be sure to add one other word to this list:

How?

How *much?* How *often?* How can we react? How can we get there from here? How can we prevent a recurrence? How can we get a piece of the market? How do we proceed?

You must ask (and answer) these kinds of questions in terms of what the audience needs and can understand. This process usually has great value in limiting the kinds of material in a presentation—and the amount of time spent explaining it.

Suppose you were going to tell the story of *Goldilocks and the Three Bears* to an audience who had never heard it. You're unsure of the information. Go back and test the foregoing questions against *Goldilocks*.

In most cases you know (or think you know) the basic subject matter for a speech, and you know where additional

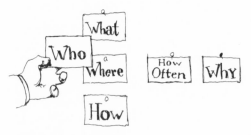

Remember the standard questions.

information can be found. (The problem is not usually the availability or scarcity of information, but knowing how to deal with an *overabundance* of it, and trying to verify its accuracy.)

One well-known and very useful technique for organizing information is to reveal *all* your key ideas so that you can see them simultaneously.

To do this, you put all your key ideas (who, what, where, how much, etc.) on note cards or scraps of paper and spread them out. Be sure to include any thoughts you have about pictures or diagrams that would simplify the story. Once you can see everything—with all the cards in front of you—you can begin to order ideas in sensible ways. It is very tough to organize your material when it's in the form of a vertical stack of papers. You can see only the top sheet of a stack.

A bulletin board comes in handy with the cards. They can be thumbtacked to the board and easily moved from one place to another. As an alternative, you can put the pieces of paper on a table or on the floor. The main thing is to be able to stand back a few feet and get a good over-all view of the various ideas you hope to present (your content), their relationship to each other (continuity), and the probable speed at which you will deliver them (pace).

The other constant in the equation is the overall time you will spend in your talk. I wish you would try to keep it short—never more than twenty or thirty minutes.

As you work with this system of spreading things out, you will begin to see new relationships that exist in your material. And, after a while, a natural organization will usually emerge—one that has a logical beginning, middle, and end.

Should this fail to happen, and you're left with a collection of unrelated facts, you may have to impose some system that will do the job *for* you.

One obvious system is a strictly *chronological* progression of events in which you say, "Number one happened first, number two happened second, number three, etc." Or you can choose a simple *cause-and-effect* presentation: "The event I'm going to tell you about took place and had an effect on the following five things." Or you might choose a *problem-solution* approach in which you present the basic problem, several possible solutions, and your final choice among those available.

When you are trying to explain a complicated issue or problem, begin by describing the *symptoms*—the effects the problem is having on people or events. Speakers usually talk about problems in an abstract way, with nothing particularly vital, personal, or immediate about them. But if you can show the impact of the problem on *people*, particularly the audience, you will provoke interest and attention in a hurry.

I can't tell you much more about it because I don't *know* much more about it. You're going to have to sweat it out. There's no magical solution.

I'll say this, though: *Use short words and short sentences.* Simplify the hell out of everything. And figure out the main ideas you really want to leave with people. I've heard teachers say that they're lucky to handle five points in an hour. So that cuts *you* down to a couple.

I'm hoping to get *one* idea across in this book: I want you to show more concern for your audience. I don't really expect you to grasp much more than that, and for that reason I've systematized all the detailed information on checklists in the back of the book. You can then tear out the checklists and carry them with you always (or loan them to somebody you assign to worry about them), and perhaps do a better job next time.

This may be *my* last Last Stand, but it's not yours.

10. Visual Things That Might Help

There are a lot of ideas about the use of, and need for, visuals, and many of them are good. The main job that visuals are supposed to do is to promote understanding. That's all—just make things easier for an audience to understand.

If I could give you only one rule to remember, it might be this one: *Use a simple visual to express a single idea.*

Most people won't do that. They clutter up their visuals with too much miscellaneous material. Visuals such as these simply masquerade as a well-prepared outline or careful work. In this case, everything the *speaker* needs to know is abridged onto one or two slides, and he or she can then talk for an hour and fifteen minutes. During this time the slide may (or may not) be explained to those members of the audience who are still awake.

The problem is not wholly the speaker's, who is merely

trying to survive, and who will try anything. They said, after all, that it was *easy*.

They said it. And let me now direct a few kind words to *them*, the folks who brought us the audiovisual "revolution."

Equipment manufacturers have done a terrific job of selling audiovisual equipment to just about everybody in the country. And the largest portion of this equipment is sitting in storerooms gathering dust because nobody knows how to use it. It was advertised to look so easy that *anybody* could do it. And it's quite true that just about anybody can turn the equipment on and off or lug it around. But very few people know how to *design* audiovisual material. Fewer still know how to produce the material once it's designed. And then we reach the real minority—those who know how to *use* the material effectively once it's produced.

It's a job that requires a high level of imagination, creative ability, experience, and skill. It also takes unusual care and a considerable amount of time. So I'm tired of the abundance of literature that explains how simple and easy everything is.

As if the audiovisual revolution weren't enough of a hoax, we now have to be very careful about a video revolution in business and industry. I suspect this new equipment will first be sold to just those places already loaded up with dusty audiovisual equipment. The same people who were deluded in the first place will now be persuaded to "upgrade" their facilities and capabilities with videotape.

Once again, the whole thing will look so effortless. *Anybody* will be able to produce TV on the first attempt. No training, planning, or thinking needed.

It is truly wonderful.

Let us advance to something much easier to understand.

Blackboards

I had intended to say that blackboards represent the one thing that audiovisual experts haven't been able to mess up. But this isn't true. The other day I tried to use a *white* blackboard. It was designed for use with greasy crayons. A marvelous idea—flawed only slightly by the fact that it didn't work. You can't see most of the colors, and you can't get the colors off the board once you get them on. A real disaster.

(I was chided recently by somebody who said that I should always say *chalk*board, since blackboards are seldom black any more, but are frequently green or some other color. I said that I would continue calling them *black*boards in the hope they would all be made that way again. Blackboards provide greater contrast.)

Anyway, a blackboard is a nice, cheap, big, simple, easy thing to use. It hasn't got a cord to trip over, and there's nothing in it that can burn out suddenly. You can put a great deal of trust in your average blackboard. (It is *possible*, I find, to tip one over, but it takes a great deal of doing.)

The blackboard is not only a handy visual device; it is also a giant prop. It provides you with a place to go (such as away from the lectern), and it gives you something to do with your hands. You can walk up to it, write something on it (or erase something from it), and walk away from it. This movement might provide the only variety in an otherwise boring and static presentation of facts.

A blackboard has a number of other advantages. You can make changes easily, there is plenty of room, and you create the illusion that the information you put on it is very current—that the data are being revealed for the first time.

Another benefit, of course, is that you can display some of your audience's thoughts on it, thereby getting more in-

Blackboards don't have cords to trip over or bulbs to burn out. They're nice.

volvement and commitment on their part. People in the audience *love* to look at their ideas written in big letters for all to see.

The best blackboard system has several boards mounted on tracks so they can roll back and forth in front of each other. Such a system enables you to prepare complex drawings or sets of figures ahead of time and roll them into view when needed.

Charts

There are two kinds of charts you may be familiar with— the stiff kind made from illustration board (these are almost impossible to carry around, particularly on airplanes). These are called flip charts. There is also a flexible paper kind that can be rolled up. These are called easel pads, and the individual sheets flip over the top like pages in a book.

Some fairly small flip charts are intended for conference room or office situations where they can be used on a table top with small audiences. Whatever their size, charts of this type are made up in advance. (I'm not going to try to tell you how to make professional-looking charts because we'd be here all night, and also because I don't particularly believe in them. If you must use charts of this sort, get somebody who knows how to do them and pay whatever you have to in order to get a good job.)

I believe in easel pads.

I believe in easel pads. An easel pad is merely a large pad of newsprint paper mounted in such a way that the individual sheets can be torn off or flipped over the top of the pad. The pad is mounted on a large tripod-type holder about 6 feet high. Easel pads can be marked on with grease pencils or with fat, juicy, felt-tip markers.

Easel pads are cheap and easy to write on. You can produce great lists of ideas and problems and then tape these lists all over the walls of a room. Such a display of thoughts (easily added to or subtracted from) greatly aids in problem solving. Important relationships between the information on the east wall and the data on the north can suddenly emerge.

The thing I like the most about both easel pads and blackboards is that the speaker generates the visual materials. This process keeps the speaker active, mobile, and animated, and lends a sense of immediacy and spontaneity to the information being presented.

All that is required of the speaker is legible handwriting—in letters large enough to be seen by the people in the back of the room. The lettering doesn't need to be artistic, merely visible and understandable.

Projectors

Two types of projectors are sold—one type for showing opaque materials and the other for transparent materials.

An opaque projector is about the size of a small elephant and just about as handy. It is designed to project pages from books, pages from reports, and a lot of other things you shouldn't be using anyway. Forget all about it.

You will encounter two basic types of projectors for

transparencies: overhead projectors and slide projectors of various sizes (the most common of which is 35mm).

Overhead projectors use a transparency about 8 by 10 inches in size that lies flat when projected. A light source underneath the transparency shines upward through it. Part of the light is collected in a periscope-like device, the optics of which direct the image onto a screen. The rest of the light goes up to the ceiling, a fact that disturbs me somewhat. Projectors of this sort also make me nervous because people won't go to the trouble of angling the screen to prevent the inevitable distortion (keystoning) of the projected image.

Overhead projectors are easily abused because the large format enables people to put enormous amounts of stuff on them, and then use them as crutches instead of as honest aids to the audience.

Two interesting features are that you can write on them with colored grease pencils, and you can produce overlays that gradually "build up" an explanation of a complicated idea. The two features can be used together by a speaker who wishes to write down a problem, discuss it, and then use an overlay to show the solution more quickly. It would

Opaque projectors are the size of small elephants (and project about as well).

be faster than taking the time to write the solution in your own hand.

There are ways of making an overhead transparency from a typewritten page, but I advise you not to use any of them. I urge you instead to join me in walking out of any presentation that uses a visual produced from a typewritten page. It can't be seen by an audience of more than two people, and *they* have to be seated within 3 feet of the screen.

With regard to audiovisual products of this kind, it's difficult to decide which is the more preposterous: the absurdity of the idea or the irrationality of the customer who would buy it.

I have nothing to say about the production of overhead transparencies. Plenty of publications have explained how easy they are to produce. Why don't you go try it and then get back to me.

35mm Slides

These have become the virtual standard for use in presentations. A few people still use lantern slides, which are about 3¼ by 4 inches. They require a projectionist, while most 35mm projectors can be operated by the speaker using a remote advance-retreat control.

I have very little to say here about photography, except to describe a paradox. A great many advertising dollars have been spent in this country to persuade people that they can take pictures. And, indeed, they *can*. There are a great many very competent picture takers in the population. A few of them even go on to become photographers. There are millions of cameras in this country.

But why is it that so few photographs (either prints or slides) are used in talks?

I'll explain why. The acquisition of a still photograph is a fairly straightforward proposition—a consideration of films, lenses, meter readings, and composition. The problem arises in the selection and organization of a *series* of pictures that is to be used to tell a *story*.

Here we bog down—not merely in pictures, but in words. It is a very complicated business that requires more care than we're usually willing to take, or more imagination than we've got. The production of an audiovisual presentation requires more than the services of a photographer or a writer. It requires somebody who can think in terms of both verbal and visual images. Very few people of this sort can be found in business communications; they are more apt to be working in television or film production.

Supposing, for the moment, that you *have* some slides, let me pass along a rule that *I* try to use. I don't like to be in the same room with a projector. Projectors belong in little projection rooms, alcoves, boxes, or someplace other than in the room where I'm trying to talk. They make noise and emit stray light, neither of which I need when I'm trying to control 100 percent of the audience's attention.

It isn't much of a hassle to put a small window in one wall of a room you use for presentations. Even if there's an office on the other side of the wall, a projector operating for a few minutes now and then won't cause any important disruption.

I will conclude this section with some tips about 35mm slide production. Use an incident light meter (and occasionally a tripod) in taking the slides, and a dissolve unit in projecting them. (A dissolve unit is used in conjunction with two projectors to make smooth transitions between slides. As the light of the first projector dims, the light of the second projector—carrying the next slide—brightens proportionally. One picture "dissolves" or overlaps into the next. This avoids the choppy effect of going to black between slides, which is characteristic with one projector.)

Other kinds of projectors include, of course, movie projectors. They *really* should be kept out of the room because the larger ones are quite noisy.

Room Lights

When you use any kind of projector, you must make provisions to darken the room. The best way to do this is to *dim* the room lights, project the material, and bring the lights back to average brightness.

Nothing is worse than throwing a switch and plunging a room into complete blackness (unless it's throwing a switch and turning all the lights back *on*, blinding everybody in the process). Rheostats don't cost very much and enable the lights to be dimmed to any comfortable level.

Things to Remember about Visuals

Despite my grumbling, I very much favor using visuals, particularly if they happen to be good and can be used gracefully. Their use must always be made to *seem* easy and simple, despite the fact that they're difficult to produce and use properly. Here are a few hot tips about production.

1. Use the simplest terms and relationships you can possibly think of.

2. Show only highlights.

3. *Never* exceed twenty-five characters (including spaces) across a visual of any kind.

4. Never exceed eight lines.

5. Omit subtitles and other extraneous words; *you're* there to pass along this information.

6. Don't use vertical printing. The audience can't turn a screen on edge as they can a page.

7. Use a minimum number of curves on graphs. Three should be the absolute limit.

8. Use the minimum number of grid lines.

9. Don't use complete sentences—only key words or phrases.

10. Allow one visual to amplify one idea.

That's enough.

Insist on one thing: that the people who design and produce your visuals attend a rehearsal in which their stuff is used. They will learn something from this expanded experience and will be able to detect problems in time to fix them. (A lot of people produce materials that they never see projected on a screen, so they think their responsibility ends at the drawing board. You must try to extend it.)

Don't use vertical printing.

Books about speaking always contain lots of detail about the visual choices the speaker can make, and provide plenty of information about charts, slides, movies, flannel boards, magnetic boards, models, video tape, filmstrips, and so forth.

Those are the conventional things.

I'm anxious to pioneer some other visual techniques such as indoor neon signs, tattooing, cave painting, theater-in-the-round, pantomime, flags and pennants, needlework, puppets, and mosaic tile.

You're welcome.

11. Some Thoughts about Your Mouth and Using It up There in Front of People

I keep harping about the need for an objective evaluation of your performance in front of an audience. You need this. And somebody (or some group of people) has to do it for you. Some people recommend using a television system in which you rehearse in front of the camera and then watch yourself on a playback monitor. I'd rather you didn't go through this process by yourself (particularly the first time or two). You should have somebody with you who can explain what's happening.

There are quite a number of things to look for in a speaker—so many, in fact, that a checklist is needed to keep track of them. One such checklist can be found at the end of this book. It doesn't differ too much from everybody else's checklist, except that it's merely named differently. These are usually called things like Speaker Analysis Form, Peer Evaluation Sheet, or—more pompously—Functional Verbal Appraisal Record.

I call mine a Grunt Detector (Checklist M).

It's divided into several basic parts, covering how you *sound*, how you *look*, and how you've managed *to get your information across*. This chapter limits itself to how you sound and look.

A few items have specifically to do with your *voice*.

Volume

The meaning of the word is easy enough to understand, but just the same, a lot of people just won't *speak up*. Why? Nobody *tells* them they aren't speaking loudly enough. A speaker *must* be heard by everybody in the audience. (That's the main reason for being there in the first place.) He or she shouldn't have to strain or waste a lot of extra energy. I've worked with actors and other people with this problem. I've taken them out into a field and made them yell. You should try it. You may get arrested, but what the hell. You'll get some idea of what you can do. (*Don't* scream as loud as you possibly can. You might ruin yourself. Just be *loud*. Some of Hamlet's soliloquies are excellent for shouting. Try it. Take a couple of cans of beer with you. Better yet, find somebody else with the same problem, and take *two* copies of *Hamlet*, plus more beer. The two of you can then stand about 50 yards apart and yell Shakespearean stuff at each other. Also, take yardsticks so that while you're yelling you can also do a little swordplay, or otherwise practice some gestures that are as broad as your voice is loud.)

Another observation is that men often have bigger, louder voices, and it's sometimes difficult in a meeting for some women (and softer-voiced men) to get a word in. It takes a little practice to learn how to raise your voice without having it crack or seem shrill and screamy. But it can be done. All you're trying to do is get attention, and once you have it, you can return to your normal speaking voice.

Practice one or two of the typical ways of getting into an open discussion (e.g., "I'd like to make a point!" or "There's something I would like to add!" or "I have something that bears on the subject!"). Then, in the actual meeting, say it in a loud, firm voice, several times if necessary.

Tone of Voice

In normal conversation you vary the tone of your voice (as well as its volume) quite naturally. Your voice changes to the same degree that your subject matter has variety. You should make an effort to bring this naturalness to the front of an audience. One of the reasons you should never *read* a speech is that there will be insufficient intonation. Unless you're a radio announcer, you'll drift into a monotone, with absolutely *no* variety.

Quality of Voice

There are ways of dealing with a voice that is too high or too low, or with the problem of talking through your nose. Speech therapists do that. I can warn you of a common problem, however, that you *can* do something about. *Don't* speak to a group if you are hoarse or your voice is raspy. It drives an audience absolutely wild, and they spend the whole time coughing and hacking trying to clear *your* throat.

Diction

You've got to enunciate. You must not mumble and continually slur words. Many of us don't enunciate as clearly as we might, and it may take a lot of practice to solve the problem. Try speaking very clearly with your teeth clenched. Recite *Mary Had a Little Lamb* with your teeth clenched—and really work those lips!

In the meantime, don't make matters worse. Don't stick a pipe or a cigar in your mouth, and don't chew gum. Also, lay off the sauce prior to a speech. You may *think* a couple of drinks will help, but they usually don't.

Breathing

This is an automatic process that normally allows us to get through a sentence without running out of breath. We do it quite naturally. There's probably something very wrong with you if you have trouble in normal conversation. *Any* time you read aloud, however, you're apt to get into trouble. In this case it is very easy to run out of breath unless the material has been written very carefully. So don't read to people. Ever.

(The one time you should read material aloud is when you're *writing*. This is a free writing tip. The next time you're working on the draft of a written piece, take it someplace and read it aloud. If you find it difficult to read out loud, then you can be sure that the reader will have trouble with it. Short sentences are both easier to say and easier to read. I learned this the hard way. In the narration recording session for the first industrial film I ever wrote, the announcer ran out of breath for the third time, threw the fifteen-page script up in the air, and walked out of the studio. The recording engineer called me on the intercom to say, "I think he had a little trouble reading your script.")

Skill in Phrasing

What does this mean? Simply that you shouldn't hang your sentences together with a lot of "and's" and "uh's." You can only get over this habit by thinking about it. If you sense you have a problem and want to do something about it, take somebody to lunch and make him or her promise to bang a fork on a glass or look cross-eyed at you every time you put two sentences together with "and" or "uh." It will probably ruin that particular relationship, but you might learn something.

(I am personally afflicted with a "you-know" problem and am apt to end most sentences with "You know?" If I had fifty cents for every time I've said that in the last six months, I wouldn't have to sit here writing this book. I'd be sitting in a sidewalk cafe on the Riviera.)

General Nervousness

If you get nervous, *never say anything about it*. To any-body. At any time. Chances are no one will ever know. We always look far less nervous than we really are. Also, don't jangle keys or change. Don't fidget. Fight to remain calm. Get more familiar with your surroundings. Get more famil-iar with your audience. Rehearse. And rehearse with people, not by yourself. Rehearse with your spouse, or a close friend. Or both. Round up some neighbors and pay them a dollar. If all else fails, talk to your dog. Chances are he'll stand very patiently and look like he's trying to understand.

Enthusiasm

If you have any interest in the subject at all, you shouldn't have any trouble communicating this interest to an audi-ence. Enthusiasm is contagious. You have to get yourself "up" for a presentation in much the same way an athlete does for a sporting event. You may find it useful to do a few mild calisthenics immediately prior to your appearance before a group—but only enough to wake you up, and not enough to make you short of breath.

Posture

You shouldn't slouch or drape yourself over lecterns and other furniture. Try to get away from lecterns. They place an obstacle between you and the audience. Force yourself to stand up straight—without looking stiff or unnatural. You may feel a little uncomfortable, but I want you to *look* good. Looks may be the only thing going for some of you.

Lecturns place an obstacle between you and the audience.

General Appearance

Dress neatly. Comb your hair. Shine your shoes. Clean your nails. Try to lower your voice a little. Don't chew gum. Don't wear clothes that are provocative or that make people laugh. Don't burst into tears. And don't drink booze because it can make your eyes look weird.

It is my opinion that women usually *look* better in front of a group than men do. (This is important when you remember that when you're up there in front of everybody, *you* are the principal visual aid.)

Men are awfully drab as a rule. Their clothes are innocuous, and most men don't wear makeup. They stand gray and haggard looking under the fluorescent lights and wonder why they're not going over like Paul Anka at the Sands. (It is, once again, my observation about competing for full attention without lights, costumes, good material, and all that other stuff.)

Women look better because they spend more time consciously planning what they're going to wear. Men put on the same clothes year after year, but women's fashions change constantly. Women have more choices to begin with: far more latitude in color, pattern, texture, design, and style. Women also know about makeup, and how much to use on what occasion.

A final advantage that women have is that they seem to have much less of a problem figuring out what to do with their hands. Most women look perfectly fine when standing in a comfortable position and not moving anything or simply standing with hands folded in front of them. This is not a matter of simply posing. It may be that women look better in this situation because their posture is often better than men. It looks nice when people stand up straight.

Facial Expression

In ordinary conversation your facial expression alters right along with changes in volume and tone of voice. It is a function of what you're saying, and you do it naturally. The more conversational you can make your presentation, the less you will have to worry about it. *Don't* try to practice in front of a mirror. You'll only mess yourself up. It's a lot like having your picture taken. You sit there and wonder what to do with your face.

Eye Contact

Look at people when you talk to them. That's not asking too much, is it? And shift your gaze and your attention among various people; don't talk to only a select one or two. Whatever you do, don't look at the ceiling. Or the back wall. Or your shoes.

Don't stare at the back wall.

Gestures

In normal conversation with people, we don't hesitate to use our hands, our arms, or our entire bodies (such as when we recount a fishing story or a golf story). But some people just can't figure out what to do with themselves in front of an audience. Their arms and hands seem to be under the control of an unseen puppeteer, or a computer in some faraway place.

Stand up for a minute. Put your hands loosely at your sides. Now put your left hand at your side and your right hand at your waist. Put your hands in back of you, holding your right wrist with your left hand. Fold your hands loosely in front of you. If you have back pockets, put your hands in them.

The next time you watch television, pay attention to what people do with their hands. Go see a silent movie.

Remember something. If you have visuals or props to handle during a presentation, be sure to rehearse with them

Pay attention to what people do with their hands.
Go see a silent movie.

well ahead of time. It will help you to use them naturally and comfortably.

I talked about gestures earlier. Do you remember exactly where? Can you turn back to it right now?

Stay on your toes!

Rapport

What was the response of your last audience to you? Was it warm? Was it cool?

You really don't have to *do* very much to get interaction with an audience. You only have to treat them with a little respect.

At one time I worked briefly with a minority group trying to get a couple of people elected to office. I kept stressing the need for a candidate who would at least be neat, clean, prompt, reasonably forceful, and possess a passing acquaintance with English grammar. But it never worked out that way.

The guy who showed up on television was inevitably late, angry, without a jacket, with tie undone, glistening with sweat, and screaming uncontrollably that he and the rest of his kind were "being robbed and conned" by the system.

What he was saying was true. The system *was* systematically robbing him and conning him.

The audience, however, wasn't about to be persuaded. When speaking to robbers and conners, you've got to be at least as clever as they are, and sensible enough to employ *their* weapons.

Dealing with Competition

There are both natural and unnatural forms of competition in meetings and other organizational settings.

Unnatural competition is that in which a person is placed at a disadvantage because of obvious discrimination (such as sex, race, or religion) or not-so-obvious discrimination (age, education, time with the company, internal politics, and so forth).

How do you deal with this in a speaking situation? It isn't simple.

If you are outnumbered in a meeting, you are bound to feel more under the gun than everybody else. This leads to real tension and the tendency to be more serious than need be. But you must try to find some middle ground, one that combines a balance of informality and sense of humor with efficiency and getting on with the job.

It's tough to come from behind and emerge from such a condition of unfair competitive disadvantage, but it's possible. It will involve working harder than everybody else and establishing a reputation for being competent, conscientious, convincing, and clear. I can't help much in this book in developing the skills of competence and conscientiousness (except perhaps to say that you should strive to do just a little more than was asked for and deliver it just a little sooner than expected).

But this book can help you some with conviction and clarity.

You will make some inroads into an unfair situation by devoting the time it takes to meet the real needs of an audience. You can become better at this than other people and you can place *them* at a competitive disadvantage.

There is a continuous opportunity for you to demonstrate that you can be less lazy, self-centered, and indifferent than those other people—and be a consistently better speaker simply by being more direct, less time-consuming, and more interesting.

This is the right time to refer back to the first line of the first preface:

"Use short sentences and be brief!"

It will help, and not just a little bit, but a lot. I promise you.

12. The Place

I mentioned this problem in Chapter 2, if you recall. I haven't changed my mind.

The place in which you choose to communicate should be a *nice* place. It should be a pleasant and interesting place. It might even be beautiful.

Most people in this country have been taught the absurd maxims "You can't judge by appearances" and "Appearances are deceiving."

Of course you can judge. You do it all the time. Appearances *aren't* deceiving. The appearance of a thing is an excellent indicator of what the thing really is. We go through life affected very largely by how things appear, and how they feel, and how they move us. We have words to describe this nonverbal sense of the rightness or wrongness of things. An old word was "vibes"; a newer one is "ambience."

The *place*, therefore, should be chosen from the standpoint of making things look easy, and comfortable, and relaxed. The environment should make the audience *feel* good. If they do, they'll be more receptive. Tension and strain will be reduced.

If the place appears gloomy and uncomfortable, the audience will be turned off. They will be further turned off if the speaker is flapping around getting things pulled together at the last minute. Scurrying around makes everybody tense (because of and *for* the speaker). This kind of nervousness spreads easily. You can add to it very easily with confusion about projectors and where to plug them in. People can run around looking for light switches. Drapes can be pulled. Screens can be noisily run up and down.

People will sit in their chairs wishing they were someplace else instead of being subjected to something that looks rat-

If the place appears gloomy and uncomfortable, the audience will be turned off.

like and frenzied—as though they had been invited to witness an animal squirming in a cage.

A meeting place should be regarded in much the same light as a living room, a clubhouse, or a private room in a good restaurant. The expectation should be created that things are going to come off easily and well, and that everybody will have a pleasant time.

In effective communications, appearances are *vital*.

Let me proceed with some ideas about changing some of the old places you've been using, or designing new ones.

One of the first things you can do, if you're afflicted with fluorescent lights, is urge people to buy *warm* white fluorescent bulbs. They will make a world of difference and everybody will look a lot better.

In designing an area for meetings and presentations, I suggest sticking with incandescent lights. For the sake of flexibility, I would put them on a lot of different circuits, and put each circuit on a dimmer. In this way you can selectively light any area you choose.

A few other simple ideas will contribute to an optimum facility:

1. More than one exit.

2. Restrooms nearby.

3. A suitable (and quiet) air conditioning and ventilation system.

4. A small projection room from which projectors shine onto a screen. I don't care much for rear-screen installations, where the people running the equipment can't see the same thing the audience are seeing. In any event, a projection room will ensure that the audience won't have to listen to the buzzing and clacking of the projectors. Once you set up a projection room, by the way, the equipment should not be moved from it. I've told you already that

audiovisual equipment isn't really portable. The less you move it, the less chance it will fail. So keep it in one place. Keep equipment covered when not in use. Clean it regularly. And keep the door locked so people won't walk off with it. Also, use *experts* for projectionists, not just anybody who happens to be standing in the hallway.

5. Rugs on the floor.

6. Table lamps.

7. Interesting colors and textures. Don't paint the place gas-chamber green or use a lot of wild patterns.

8. Variable lighting. Arrange it so you can darken the room. Have window drapes backed with a lightproof material. (On the other hand, make the windows large enough so you can admit plenty of sunlight when it's available.)

9. No phones.

10. Sliding corkboard panels that move to one side to reveal a blackboard.

11. High enough ceilings.

12. Good acoustics.

13. Cleanliness and order at all times.

14. Comfortable places to sit. Let me speak about this important point at greater length. A lot of mistakes are made in this area: one of the gravest blunders is installing rows of seats that can't be moved. I can understand the need to do this in a movie theater, but most other places should have movable chairs. In a bolted-down row of seats, the only people you can talk to (by craning considerably) are those to your immediate left or right. Chairs in a meeting area should be comfortable and movable, and the room should permit a great many chair arrangements—big circles, small circles, horseshoes, and ovals—any way that meets the exact needs of the group and the subject to be discussed.

Don't install rows of seats that can't be moved.

15. No tables. Tables inhibit the communication of ideas, and large conference tables actually help to proliferate garbage. I'm sure you've noticed that people bring lots of photocopies of things to meetings held around a large table. They know that each person will have a large piece of table to *store* things—tablets and pencils, notes, reports, and photocopies of all the things that other people brought. Soon the place on the table in front of the person becomes more important than the actual person. Nobody pays any attention to the person's *mind*, or *telling* things—they merely pass down reams of paper to the person's chunk of table. Each person later wanders away with all the paper and a strange mixture of certainty and confusion—the certainty that it's not going to be read, and the confusion about throwing it away. So it gets filed.

Meetings should be held without anything that can act as camouflage or armor. People should meet once in a while without pencils or paper—or even pockets, such as outdoors in swimming suits.

It would improve communications.

In the course of consulting, I've seen a lot of *places*—special conference rooms and presentations areas. One of the most elaborate was a board of directors room that must have cost a half million dollars. It was a beautiful room with three or four kinds of lighting and an enormous floor-to-ceiling window that ran the entire length. A group of us assembled to watch a motion picture. About three minutes into it, the projector suddenly developed an appetite for film.

After chewing up several feet, the projector stopped. It was rethreaded and restarted. It ate some more. Several other attempts were made in the next fifteen minutes. They all failed. The projectionist reported that the problem had to do with the fact that the film had splices in it. But this is nonsense; a projector in good repair can project spliced film.

They had no other projector. They had no other copy of the film, even though it had been produced at great expense to describe precisely the operation of the company.

After giving up in disgust, the projectionist went away without turning up the room lights. We sat in the gloom as the speaker stammered about the content of the film, as well as he could remember it.

It was a complete disaster. And unforgivable.

13. A Short Note about Meetings

Three kinds of meetings immediately come to mind. I will list them in the order of their importance: (1) things-are-going-to-hell meetings, (2) planning-ahead meetings, and (3) ritual meetings.

You are invited to a things-are-going-to-hell meeting.

The purpose of the first type of meeting is to try to figure out why things are going to hell. Sometimes (rarely) things will fall apart for sudden and unpredictable reasons. More often, things go to pieces because people didn't do what they were expected to do or promised to do. It is difficult to conduct a meeting of this sort because everybody wants to talk at once—to explain his or her point of view and make appropriate excuses for whatever it is that's going haywire. It is also typical in a meeting such as this for people to have wildly different meanings for the same word. Vocabulary is one of the first problems to attack. A meeting such as this is required, in most cases, because of one or more of the following conditions:

1. No action is being taken.
2. Part, but not all, of a desired action is being taken.
3. The wrong action is being taken.
4. The right action is being taken, but too soon or too late.
5. The wrong *version* of the right action is being taken. (Last year's procedure is being employed—the one in the blue cover. This year's color is yellow.)

The second type, planning-ahead meetings, are less strained. The pressures are less great. People are more willing to take their turns at speaking and are usually better prepared.

The last type, ritual meetings, are purely ceremonial. They exist because they have always existed. Friday afternoon's meeting is Friday afternoon's meeting. There are a lot of ritual meetings in universities and other aging businesses.

A ritual meeting looks very active, and things *seem* to be happening. Three things *are:* (1) issues or problems are identified; (2) the issues or problems are put into some kind of order (*prioritized*, I think the word is); and then (3) because all the time is used up, no action is taken or even proposed. The agenda of the next meeting is precisely the same. Usually, the same issues and problems will be identified, but, because of the simple passage of time, the priorities will have changed. These types of meetings are strictly democratic; everybody agrees (even in disagreeing), and no action is ever taken.

If you feel compelled to have a meeting in which you actually wish to get something accomplished, then keep some of the following things in mind:

1. Try to put together an agenda so that people will know, in advance, what you're trying to do (and what is expected of them).

2. Try, when the meeting starts, to keep the proceedings to the point and not let discussion stray into other issues, especially those which are completely unrelated.

3. Try to make possible an environment in which new information can be added and new ideas can be tested.

4. Try to discover underlying causes and relationships.

5. Encourage people to discuss their opinions and attitudes (which might be quite different from the "facts" of the matter).

6. Agree on the meanings of words.

7. Develop a written record of what happened (on easel pads).

There are some things you can do *ahead* of the event, such as the production of handouts and charts or other visuals. Also, as with any other speaking situation, it is well to get to the room ahead of time so that you can be familiar with it and make sure that everything is ready.

After the event, review immediately your written record of the meeting, plus any other notes you can add. Most importantly, *follow up on any of the commitments* that were made during the meeting by you or by anybody else. If people have agreed to take action, then record it and measure it (otherwise it's just another ritual or ceremonial meeting and it will tend to perpetuate itself).

The reasons that most committee efforts fail is that the committee itself is too unwieldy and cumbersome to take action as a body. Small groups of two or three people, however, can agree to take action and succeed in doing so.

14. Prior To

This chapter is divided into three subparts entitled *Well Prior To* (meaning more than a week), *Somewhat Prior To* (meaning two or three days), and *Immediately Prior To* (meaning minutes).

Well Prior To

You can score extra points well before your talk ever starts. One of the first, and probably the most important, is with *invitations*.

For fast, thrown-together meetings, a phone call will do just fine. You can talk to people and advise them of where and when and what to expect.

For a more formal kind of presentation, or one in which all or part of the audience is unknown to you, you should send a written notification such as a memo.

A memo can serve a variety of purposes, a couple of which are political, but which mostly do an honest job of telling the audience what to expect.

Such a memo should include the place the presentation will be held, the date and the time, and an agenda of what will be included (with some sense of how long a period of time it will take). The memo can also briefly describe something of the subject matter, and the credentials of the speaker.

Such a memo may also suggest that the audience bring something *to* the meeting, such as past records, notes, or ideas.

Determine well ahead of time whether the meeting will be informal. A formal meeting is one in which you do not expect much in the way of audience participation. You progress through your material without any questions from the audience. If any questions are accepted, they wait until the end. An *informal* presentation invites participation from the audience at any time.

Somewhat Prior To

Get onto the stage or into the front of the presentations area. Walk around the stage and get familiar with it. Handle the microphones. Work with blackboards, easels, and props. Check the lights, and ensure that the right kinds of projection equipment will be on hand when needed.

The main thing at this point is to rehearse adequately. Without rehearsal you will find that words don't come out as easily as you expected them to. You fumble. You go into your famous "uh," "ah," and "hmmmm" number.

You try to use the blackboard and the chalk explodes. The easels fall over. You drop things. And trip over cords.

Rehearse. Please. Rehearse.

And each time these petty annoyances take place, you lose more of your train of thought. Finally you lose it altogether and you stop dead. Stunned. Silent.

Rehearse sufficiently and you'll not only get through your talk successfully, but you'll be able to answer questions more easily. It often happens that rehearsal in front of another person will show up gaps in your information or holes in your logic.

Immediately Prior To

Go someplace and loosen up your voice by singing, shouting, or speaking in an overly loud voice. Go "Mi, mi, mi, mi," or "Fa, fa, fa, fa" a few times. Get your voice out of your normal conversational register. Also wave your arms around and perhaps jump up and down a few times.

By getting yourself physically up for the meeting, you also raise your emotional and intellectual levels.

Go to the bathroom. Get a drink of water. Focus your attention on your subject matter and keep it there for a few minutes prior to your talk. If you're comfortable about everything, you'll be able to chat with a few people beforehand. If you're not quite that comfortable, concentrate up to the last minute.

Then go out there and let them have it.

Go out there and let them have it!

15. During

The trouble with making a speech is that so many things are happening at once. You have to be concerned with your material, yourself, your audience, and the environment (plus all their complex interrelationships). A book can discuss these aspects one at a time, but *you* have to endure them simultaneously (and in an environment that is usually neither friendly nor familiar).

Your material has its own special set of requirements. It has to be unfolded in a certain way to make any sense. And it must keep the audience interested. While visual materials may aid in the understanding of the information, they also pose problems in setup and handling.

The problems *you* face as an audiovisual aid have been discussed in detail. They include how you look and sound, whether you're interested or not, excited or not, nervous or not.

The audience have their worries that must be calculated. They may be tired, hungry, thirsty, bored, angry, or just badly in need of a break.

The environment contributes to audience comfort, but poses a set of potential dangers to you. Equipment fails. Jackhammers start up outside. Things go haywire.

Use the checklists at the end of this book. They will help to minimize the number of outside things that can go wrong (or simply will never be assured of going right until somebody devotes attention to them). You should improve your next presentation by at least 50 percent by worrying about just a few of the *little* things.

While you're up there in front of everybody juggling all these considerations, you must also watch the audience very carefully and try to react to what they're doing (or failing to do).

If you've made an honest effort to get organized and can keep your talk as short as possible, chances are you won't bore them.

If it looks like you've lost them, you should summarize quickly and sit down.

Keep your eye on people. You have to be completely blind to avoid seeing obvious signs of boredom and nervousness. They include:

1. Not looking at you
2. Cleaning fingernails
3. Doodling
4. Yawning
5. Passing notes and repressing laughter
6. Looking intently at the wall behind you
7. Looking out the window
8. Jerking suddenly upright after having dozed off
9. Reading other material

Watch for subtle signs of boredom in the audience.

10. Outright sleeping

A miserable trick to play is identifying somebody who is obviously not paying attention and firing a question at him: "That *is* the right number, isn't it, Ed?"

That may galvanize the audience for just a little while. But not for long.

16. After

After your talk you may wish to distribute handouts that cover the highlights of your material. You may also want to lead a discussion that can decide on action to take now that you've *made* the presentation. In any event, you must be prepared to answer questions or objections.

Even though these things take place *after* your talk, you should mention them ahead of time. It will make the audience more attentive if they know their participation is expected at the end.

You perform a real service if you indicate to an audience that you will provide handouts of the highlights of your talk. It relieves them of the need to take notes. You can't expect them to remember large volumes of information anyway.

You should provide handouts for the audience if you have been talking about complex data such as figures, tables, graphs, or drawings. They may consist of some of the actual visuals used (but in a modified form to include titles and legends) or other interpretive or explanatory notes.

The handout should meet these simple tests: Is this important to an understanding of my ideas? Will it help to achieve my objective?

Above all, distribute handouts *after* you've said what you wanted to say, not before. If you distribute a handout before you speak, you invite the audience to read rather than listen to you. They will also rattle the paper.

Having made the presentation, you will also want to deal with the question of *follow-through*, to ensure that some appropriate action takes place as a result of your presentation.

This can be a two-part proposition. You can tell the audience, or selected members within that audience, what you expect *them* to do, establishing dates and deadlines by which work or effort is expected. You may also wish to tell the audience what *you* intend to do, and by when. (Living up to that commitment may be the determining factor in the credibility of your presentation—in other words, "You told us what you were going to do, and you *did* it.")

The last of your after-speech considerations is your ability to handle the questions or objections that may arise at the end of the presentation.

You should take some special pains to provide whatever backup material you might need to provide proofs, verifications, or explanations.

If you really get pinned to the wall, you may wish to get out of it by using (very firmly) such things as:

1. *"To be quite frank with you, I don't have that information with me. I'll have to get back to you."*

2. *"Since that information isn't of particular interest to the entire group, we'll discuss it at some point after the meeting."*

There are two great all-time stratagems to employ when you're asked a question and need some time to think of an answer.

The first requires a lot of nerve and stage presence. You listen to the question and then say, "I'll have to think about that for a minute."

Then you stand there and think about it for a minute. It drives an audience up the wall to see somebody that cool.

The other thing to do (and probably better) is to *rephrase the question or the objection*. Very casually say, "Do I understand you to say that you think . . . ," and then provide a somewhat longer version of the question or objection.

While you're stalling this way, you have a chance to think of an answer. You can also count on gaining time because the original questioner will inevitably want to embellish your embellishment of the original questions. This, of course, gives you a chance to attack the later embellishment instead of dealing with the real issue. (You are bound to find some small error in judgment or logic by comparing the two statements.)

In some cases the listener will develop the question into a statement, or even a minor address. In either case you're clearly out of trouble.

Like any good salesperson, you've got to minimize objections and capitalize on any points on which you and the audience can reach agreement. You've got to get their heads nodding affirmatively and keep them that way.

As I've tried to explain, the process of getting people to

nod agreement begins well ahead of the talk, with an intelligent invitation and an intelligent explanation of what is expected of them. Everything you do contributes to ultimate success and is worth the investment of time or expenditure of energy.

17. Much Later

Checklist M in this book is called a Grunt Detector. It can be used by those who review your next appearance in front of an audience.

(I say *those* because it may be easier for you to find a *group* of people to give the forms to, rather than one individual who might feel awkward about it. Give copies to several people and let them return the forms without their names on them. In this way you can average the inputs and perhaps arrive at a more honest appraisal of yourself.)

Within Checklist M are buried the following questions that should be asked after *any* speech.

    1. Did it get off the ground either immediately or eventually?

    2. Did it consider mutual interests, aspirations, and points of view?

    3. Did it use understandable language?

4. Did it *say* anything?

5. Was it worth the *time?*

6. Was it thoughtfully prepared (to the point where there could be no misunderstanding)?

7. Did it begin to open two-way communication or stimulate discussion?

8. Did it pave the way for something to happen? For a course of action to emerge? For commitment?

9. Did it seem responsible for eventual outcome, or was it merely talk?

10. Did it persuade?

It will be difficult for you to estimate the success of *your* next talk by using these questions, but you can apply them to the next presentation you attend. Carry this book to the meeting and grade the speaker.

The Checklists

No claim is made for the completeness of these lists, so *add* to them. Their purpose is to try to make you *think* a little bit, and consider a few more things about a presentation than just your mouth.

Checklist A

Things That Are True about Speeches, But Sound Dumb

1. In order to communicate ideas to people, we must:
   (a) Have a clearly defined subject
   (b) Select those facts that will make the subject understandable and convincing to the audience
   (c) Arrange the facts and ideas in an effective manner

2. An audience's ability to understand is affected by:
   (a) The vocabulary we choose to use
   (b) The style of presentation
   (c) The way the information is organized
   (d) The general abstractness of the subject
   (e) Idea density

3. Long words are harder to understand than short words.

4. Long sentences are more difficult to understand than short ones.

5. You can't expect to present a lot of ideas in a short period of time. You will bog down in irrelevant details.

6. Speeches are a good idea because people are more apt to act on something they *hear* rather than on something they *read*.

7. When we watch and listen to something, we are sensitive to the content, but also to the way the speaker *looks*. And we respond to the manner and delivery.

8. Somebody told me that after a talk people will remember about 60 percent of the content. After eight hours, they'll remember somewhere between half and a third. (This means that after about seven weeks, you'll not only have forgotten the content of this book, you won't even remember where you *put* it.)

Checklist B

Questions to Ask about Your Audience

1. Do they already know something about the subject?

2. Does each individual in the audience know as much as everybody else?

3. Are they interested in the subject?

4. What is their level of understanding?

5. Are there reasons *why* they should be interested?

6. Do they have attitudes about the subject?

7. How much background will you have to provide in order for them to understand the current situation?

8. What are their opinions? About the subject? About the speaker?

9. Has anybody else ever talked to them about it?

10. Is there some way to communicate with them that has been successful in the past?

11. What are their real needs in this case?

12. Will they be able to see connections between what you're saying and what they're doing (living, thinking, or understanding)?

13. Will they be a friendly audience?

14. Will they be open-minded?

15. Are they apt to be hostile?

16. Do you expect them to ask questions?

17. Do you expect them to raise objections?

18. Do you have any idea about the things that might antagonize them? Taboo words? Taboo subjects? Allusions? Something in the past? Gestures?

19. Do they know anything about you?

20. Do they know what level of responsibility or authority you bring to the problem?

21. What is *their* rank? Below, equal with, or higher than yours? Does this have a bearing on your subject matter or style of delivery?

22. Do you think they will expect a formal talk or an informal one?

23. Is there anything special about the audience?

24. Is there anything special about the place?

25. Is there anything special about the time (the time of day, week, month, or year)?

26. Is there some connection between you and them?

27. Is there some connection between your organization (company, church, political party) and theirs?

28. What benefits might accrue to them?

29. When might they accrue?

30. Are there disadvantages to the audience?

31. What benefits accrue to *you* by addressing this particular audience?

32. Are there *dis*advantages to you?

Checklist C

The Room and Making the Audience Comfortable in It

1. Remember to invite them to the room or the place.

2. Have comfortable chairs to sit in.

3. Arrange the chairs suitably.

4. Make sure that you have the right equipment.

5. Make sure the equipment is in good working order.

6. Make sure that the person operating it is competent.

7. Assure that there will be a minimum of distractions. (If you're making a presentation in an office, make sure that telephone calls are held.)

8. Provide name cards and place cards when appropriate.

9. Make sure the room has adequate ventilation, particularly when you know that cigar smokers will be present.

10. Make sure the room is suitable from the standpoint of size, number of people in the audience, material to be presented, and so forth. Will the people in the back be able to see?

11. Set aside enough time for breaks. Let people move around, go to the bathroom, etc.

12. Where *are* the bathrooms?

13. See that there are enough electrical oulets and that they are suitable for the load.

14. Arrange for blackboards and easels.

15. Find a room that is good acoustically. Hard ceilings and walls reflect sounds and make hearing difficult because of echoes. Curtains and carpeting help.

16. If using projectors, be sure to use a screen and not a wall. Even a white wall will absorb too much light. Beaded screens are best, but they require a certain angle of viewing. (This

angle is generally within 20 degrees on either side of the projection axis—which means that half the room will be dead space.)

17. Also, when using projectors, allow 6 square feet per viewer, and don't put anybody closer to the screen than twice the width of the picture. (The viewer should be at least 8 feet back from a 4-foot picture.)

Checklist D

An Alphabetical List of Items to Remember If You Ever Go Outside Your Own Place

1. acoustics
2. agenda
3. ash trays
4. audiovisual person
5. badges
6. bulletin board in lobby
7. ceiling height
8. chalk
9. checkroom facilities
10. cleanliness
11. coffee breaks
12. confirmations
13. conflicting concurrent meetings
14. cost
15. date of activities
16. direction signs (in lobby and elsewhere)
17. easels
18. entertainment
19. flannel board
20. flip charts
21. floor size
22. hotel reservations
23. lectern (and light)
24. lighting
25. location of windows
26. meal planning and scheduling
27. microphones
28. models and samples
29. name cards
30. optical pointer
31. parking
32. PA system
33. pencils
34. place cards
35. pointer
36. power available
37. projection equipment
38. projection facilities
39. projection personnel
40. recreation
41. registration
42. rest rooms
43. room signs
44. soundproofing
45. spare bulbs for projectors
46. transportation
47. ventilation
48. water pitchers and glasses
49. writing accessories (grease pencils, felt-tip pens)
50. writing pads

Checklist E
Putting Together a New Act

1. Begin by taking the time to write a one-paragraph description of what you intend to do. You may have to answer questions such as: When did the problem start, and why? What are the key parts of the subject matter and what are the subordinate parts? What is the influence? What is the outlook? How much is involved? How often is it happening?

2. Accumulate data on cards and spread the cards out in one place so you can see all the key ideas at one time.

3. If no organization becomes immediately apparent, try one of the following systems of presenting information: (*a*) chronological, (*b*) cause-and-effect, or (*c*) problem-solution.

4. At the *beginning* of the speech you may choose to: (*a*) acquaint the audience with your qualifications or interests in dealing with the problem, (*b*) arouse interest in the subject, (*c*) orient people to the problem, and (*d*) direct attention to some specific issues.

5. In the *middle* of the talk you might: (*a*) describe the symptoms of the problem and the influence it seems to be having on people and events, (*b*) describe the problem, (*c*) explain the constraints on the solution, (*d*) summarize various possible solutions, and (*e*) recommend the best alternative or combination of alternatives.

6. *End* by summarizing the main ideas, solutions, or opportunities that have emerged in your analysis. Recommend action, even if it is only in the form of further discussion.

7. Go back to point 1 of this checklist and read the first sentence again. That is a very useful idea indeed.

Checklist F

Using Visuals

Common sense will tell you that visuals are used to:

1. Show how things look (as in photos)

2. Show how things work (as in diagrams or models)

3. Show how things relate to each other (as in organization charts)

4. Show important information such as key words or key numbers

Checklist G

Designing Visuals

1. Use simple terms and relationships.

2. If a visual doesn't explain something better than words, it shouldn't be used.

3. A visual should never exceed twenty-five characters across (counting spaces).

4. It should have a minimum number of lines, certainly no more than eight.

5. Only highlights should be shown.

6. A complete sentence should never be used, only key words or phrases.

7. Cover only one idea per visual, and don't dwell on it for more than a couple of minutes at most.

8. On graphs, use a minimum number of curves, never exceeding three.

9. Use a minimum number of grid lines.

10. Eliminate supplementary notes.

11. Omit subtitles.

12. Never use vertical printing.

13. A visual for a presentation should contain far less information than an illustration for a report or a handout.

Checklist H
How to Handle a Group Discussion

1. Develop an outline of the topics to be discussed and the sensible order in which they should be discussed. Stick to the outline.

2. If such an outline has not been developed ahead of time, begin the discussion by developing one with the audience. Display the ideas prominently on a blackboard or on pages from an easel pad.

3. In case there is insufficient comment, come prepared with appropriate or provocative questions.

4. Don't allow people to get into time-consuming and fruitless arguments.

5. Try to show the relationship of the topics to one another.

6. Try to show the relationship of the topics to objectives.

7. Shut off discussion when a topic has been sufficiently discussed.

8. Try to get participation from everybody present.

9. Encourage members to share experiences or ideas.

10. Don't let one or two people dominate the discussion.

11. Develop a course of action.

12. Prepare for action to take place. Find volunteers to take the next action steps. Failing that, make assignments.

13. Be responsible for the eventual outcome.

Checklist I

What to Make a Speech About

This is a checklist for people who are forced into making a speech, but don't know what to make it about. It seems ludicrous perhaps to think that such a thing could ever happen to you, but let me assure you that the odds are closer to one-in-two than they are to one-in-a-million. The following are guaranteed to work.

1. Talk about the developments in the technology, research, or administration connected with any subject you know about. (To arrive at a title for your presentation, merely take the key subject, add a colon, and attach the words "problems and prospects." It will work for anything: *Tuna Packing: Problems and Prospects.*)

2. Talk about problems and solutions (problems with your organization, its goals, its people, its budget, its deadlines, its prospects, etc.).

3. Talk about the *applications* of whatever it is you do, sell, or plan.

4. Talk about innovations made recently (or since the beginning of World War II).

5. Provide instruction about the use of a device, a system, or a concept.

6. Talk about the need for quality control.

7. Talk about new procedures or invite the audience to help you develop some new procedures.

8. Decide to *evaluate* something. Or somebody. Get audience participation.

9. Formulate a policy or *plan* something.

10. Invite the audience to help you consider some new ways of developing enthusiasm or improving morale.

Checklist J

Why You Should Rehearse

1. To gain enough familiarity that the right words come out effortlessly and naturally

2. To allow the easy use of visuals

3. To look and feel more comfortable

4. To stay on the track and finish on time

5. To make it easier for you to answer questions and to anticipate them

6. Because rehearsal may show up some gaps in your information or holes in your logic

Checklist K
Using Projection Equipment

1. Make sure it is set up before the event.

2. Make sure that it works.

3. Make sure that it has the right lens.

4. Make sure *you* have the right film or slides.

5. Check the seats (by sitting in them) to make sure that everybody will be able to see.

6. If you need help with the lights, pick somebody ahead of time.

7. After its use, leave the equipment alone until after the entire presentation. Don't bother about rewinding film or putting slides away.

8. Thread the motion picture projector before the event.

9. Prefocus the projector and set the volume level.

10. Have a spare bulb.

11. Know how to change the bulb.

12. Know how to remove a slide that sticks.

13. Remember that sound projectors need time to warm up.

14. Turn off the projector at the end so that people don't have to look at a dazzling white screen.

Checklist L

Things to Do with Your Hands

1. Let your left hand fall at your side. Pick up a pencil and keep it in your right hand. Do not let that hand fall below your waist.

2. Hold some 3- by 5-inch cards in your left hand. Gesture, if you can, with your right hand.

3. Hold some 3- by 5-inch cards in your left hand and a felt-tip marker in your right hand. At some point in your talk, tap the cards with the marker.

4. Take a pencil or pen from a blouse or shirt pocket and gesture with it. Keep both hands above your waist.

5. At some point, take off your glasses and gesture with them.

6. Sometime during your talk, take off your glasses and clean them with a hankderchief or tissue. Gesture with them in the process.

7. Fold a blank piece of paper twice. Hold it in front of you with both hands. Occasionally gesture with it with your right hand. Do not let either hand fall below your waist.

8. Bend your left arm 90 degrees at the elbow and form the left hand into a loose fist. Place this hand over your navel and leave it there during the course of your talk. Gesture with your right hand.

9. Fold your arms; then make gestures by placing your left hand under your right elbow (thereby supporting it) and gesturing with your right arm extended. Point your finger.

10. Put a pencil in one hand and some 3- by 5-inch cards in the other. Do not let either hand fall below your waist.

11. Pick up a 12-inch ruler from the table. Use it in your right hand to gesture with, particularly to make an aggressive point.

12. Have a yardstick nearby. Use it as a prop. It can be held in one hand or both hands (and used as a rifle, a pointer, etc.).

13. Sit on the edge of the table (directly over one of the legs) and put one foot on the floor. Put your left arm on your lap and gesture with your right hand.

14. Pick up three pencils and hold them in your left hand. Then, at some point, transfer them to your right hand. Later, tap your left hand with the three pencils. At no point let your hands fall below your waist.

15. Pick up some 3- by 5-inch cards and hold them with both hands (both elbows bent, with the cards held about an inch above your navel). At some point, leave your left hand at your navel and gesture, cards in hand, with your right.

16. Pick up a roll of tape or some other object and keep it in your left hand. Gesture with your right. Do not let either hand fall below your waist.

17. Keep a pencil or pen in your right hand and do not let that hand fall below your waist.

18. Pick up your briefcase with your left hand, cross the room, and open the door with your right hand. Turn back and wave good-bye with your right hand.

Checklist M

Grunt Detector

Truth Index

1. Truthful and explicit.
2. A few things didn't ring true.
3. Suspicious.
4. I think you lied and I think they knew it.
5. Propaganda throughout.

Confusion Scale

1. It was perfectly clear and confused nobody.
2. Once in a while things were a little hard to follow.
3. There were some rough places, such as: _____

_____

_____

4. The whole thing was hazy.
5. I'm afraid it was a fiasco.

Length

1. A little too short. You could have developed some of the ideas a little further.
2. Just right. Everybody felt good.
3. A little long, but OK.
4. It dragged in a lot of places.
5. Altogether too long. No doubt about it. You spent too much time on: _____

_____

_____

Visuals

1. They were pertinent, easy to see, and easy to understand.
2. They were not always easy to understand.
3. It was hard to see them.
4. They were too complicated.
5. They were unnecessary.

Interest Level

1. Very high. Very interesting at all points.
2. Fascinating in places. Slow in others.
3. Somewhat slow throughout.
4. Rather dull.
5. A real exercise in daylight bombing.

Volume

1. It was OK all the time.
2. It was OK most of the time.
3. You have some kind of a problem.

Tone of Voice

1. Very natural.
2. As natural as *you* ever get.
3. Spotty.
4. Monotonous.

Diction

1. Every word clear as a bell.
2. A few words were slurred.
3. You may have to give this some serious thought.
4. We should maybe find some kind of a doctor.

Breathing

1. The breathing is OK.
2. The breathing is not OK.

Speed and Pacing

1. It went very well. Very natural.
2. There were places where things slowed down, like at:

_____

_____

_____

3. There were places where you went a little too fast, like at:

_____

_____

_____

4. It was too slow overall.
5. It was too fast overall.

Skill in Phrasing

1. Very good.
2. Pretty good.
3. Fair.
4. Lousy.

General Nervousness

1. Like an actor, already.
2. Some nervousness at the beginning only.
3. Edgy all the way through, but OK.
4. Nervousness apparent to audience.
5. You looked bad, kid.
6. Get out of show business.

Enthusiasm

1. A little too much.
2. Damned good.
3. Damned average.
4. Marginal.
5. Nonexistent.

Posture

1. Good/natural.
2. You slouched a couple of times.
3. Sloppy.
4. Ludicrous.

General Appearance

1. Great.
2. Snappy.
3. Flashy.
4. Your father took nice care of his clothes.
5. If you're going to wear white socks, then remember to carry a tennis racket.

Facial Expression

1. Good.
2. Indifferent.
3. *What* face?

Eye Contact

1. You looked at everybody. Good.
2. Reasonably good.
3. You tended to look in the same place all the time.
4. Bad. You looked at the floor all the time. (Or you looked at the _____ all the time.)

Gestures

1. Very natural.
2. Generally pretty good.
3. You have trouble with your _____ .
4. Weak.
5. None I could see.

Knowledge of Subject

1. Good.
2. Fair.
3. Not so good.
4. No good at all.

Delivery

1. You simplified complicated ideas.
2. You complicated simple ideas.
3. I really don't know *what* the hell you did.

Grammar

1. You've got it.
2. You ain't entirely got it.

It Started Off

1. Great.
2. Slow, but picked up.
3. Slow, but then went to hell.
4. The way it ended. With a thud.

The Language You Used Was

1. Understandable in every case. Appropriate.
2. Confusing in one or two cases.
3. Vague.
4. Too complicated.
5. Lithuanian?

The Presentation Said

1. Quite a bit.
2. Something.
3. Not much.
4. Very little.
5. Nothing new.
6. Nothing at all.

Was It Worth the Time?

1. Yes, well worth it.
2. Yeah, for the most part.
3. I don't know. Half and half.
4. No, quite frankly it wasn't.

Did It Establish Two-Way Communications?

1. Sure.
2. Sort of.
3. No.
4. What was the question?

Did It Seem Responsible for Eventual Outcome?

1. Very much.
2. I guess so.
3. I couldn't tell.
4. Obviously not.

Was Anybody Persuaded?

1. All of them.
2. A bunch.
3. A few.
4. One or two.
5. None.
6. One guy said he was going to defect somewhere in South America.

Checklist N

What Happened?

1. Did people understand?

2. Were people convinced?

3. Did they participate?

4. Is there going to be some outcome?

5. If you really *expect* some outcome, have you thought about any of the following possible requirements:
   a. A change in people's behavior
   b. Ways of measuring progress
   c. Scheduling or phasing
   d. Forecasting
   e. Objectives/strategy
   f. Ample budget
   g. New equipment
   h. Additional people
   i. Training
   j. Impact on other parts of the organization
   k. Logistics

(Add some things of your own to this list.)

Checklist O

A 22-Point Fantasy

Imagine this: You scheduled a very big and very elaborate series of meetings and presentations. You asked people to fly in from all over. You made every effort you could to persuade them. Two days after the event you receive the following note:

I've never been to a better meeting than yours, and I've stopped to analyze the reasons why I thought it was so good:

1. *It was great, after that long flight, to be met at the airport and not have to worry about luggage, or the hassle of renting a car or finding other transportation.*

2. *It was a pleasant surprise to go into the hotel and be told that I was expected and that registration had already been taken care of.*

3. *The desk clerk handed me the four things you'd prepared: (a) the services and hours of the hotel, (b) the various services (including recreation and entertainment) in the community, (c) a note that explained precisely where I was supposed to go for the first meeting (plus how long it would be and what I could expect), and (d) background information on the speakers and, flatteringly enough, information about us participants.*

4. *It was a nice touch to go to the room and find a small basket of fruit, something interesting to read, and something to drink. It satisfied the three great needs of a late-arriver: a small hunger, boredom, and the need of a drink.*

5. *The room was comfortable, clean, and everything worked.*

6. *The hotel food was great and the service excellent.*

7. *I found the first meeting without any difficulty.*

8. *The seats were comfortable and so was the room. It was well ventilated and air-conditioned.*

9. *The meeting started precisely on time, and was run by*

people with knowledge and enthusiasm. They set the stage (and the pace) for the rest of the day.

10. I was surprised at how smoothly they used the visuals in their presentations. Usually you have to put up with the noise of a projector, a bumbling projectionist, and a lot of delay getting started. Everything was well organized ahead of time.

11. There were no distractions outside the meeting room. That was a relief. Things went smoothly.

12. Even the coffee break looked like it had been planned like a military operation. It went quickly and smoothly, with no hassles or delays.

13. The arrangement of the room had been worked out so that it was possible to participate and interact (both with the speakers and with other members of the audience).

14. Lunch went well. We were promptly and efficiently served, and had no trouble keeping to the meeting schedule for the afternoon.

15. Rest breaks were conveniently planned throughout the day.

16. It was a good idea to distribute handouts at the end of the sessions. The summaries and outlines will be very useful in remembering what you said.

17. Despite the number of people involved in the presentations, they were united in purpose and intent. It was well organized.

18. There were smooth transitions between sessions.

19. The presentations were polished and well-executed.

20. At the end of the day, I felt I had participated in something useful and interesting, not merely been subjected to something (or, worse yet, conned).

21. *There was none of the usual flap at checkout time. You had prearranged everything.*

22. *It was comfortable being taken to the airport.*

I have seldom been treated with as much consideration.

Index

Pictures, using, 64
Planning a talk, 91
Plaza Hotel experience, 21–22
Pomeroy, Pamela, 60
Posture, 73, 121
Preparations:
    Checklist O, 125
    of professionals, 5
Preparing everything carefully, 125
Presentations, prior to, 90
Problem-solution presentation, 54
Problems audiences say they have, 32
Problems speakers say they have, 32
Projection equipment, how to use, 116
Projectors, 61
    use of, how much and where, 108
Props, 117

Quality of voice, 70

Rapport with audience, 77
Rehearse, why you should, 115
Relationships and connections, 47
Replacement, finding a, 8, 9
Restaurants, 12
Rheostats for lights, 65
Room arrangements, 83
    Checklist C, 107
Room lights, 65
Room size, 107

Seating, 83
Self-confidence, 36
Show business, 16, 17
Size of room, 107
Skill in phrasing, 71, 121
Slides, 35mm, 63
Specialized language, 46

Speeches:
    the beginning, 110
    components of, 20
    the end, 110
    the middle, 110
    subject matter for, 114
Speed and pacing, 43, 120
Stage fright, 34
Subject, knowledge of, 46
Subject matter for speeches, 114
Symptoms-cures presentation, 54

Taboo words, 48
Talking too fast, 43
Technical terms, 46
Television, watching yourself on, 14, 15
Themes for speeches, 114
35mm slides, 63
Time limits, keeping within, 39
Tone of voice, 70, 120
TV, watching yourself on, 14, 15

Ventilation, 107
Vertical printing (no!), 112
Visual-aid advice, 65
Visuals, 56
    evaluating, 119
    highlights of, 112
    how to design, 112
    number of lines on, 112
    what they do, 111
Voice, tone and quality of, 70, 120
Volume, 69, 120

Watchers, Americans as, 7
Where to talk, 81
Winging it, 18, 19
Words, choice of, 104
Working on a stage, 18